THE ILLUSTRATED HISTORY OF MILITARY VEHICLES

THE ILLUSTRATED HISTORY OF MILITARY VEHICLES

Ian V. Hogg and John Weeks

Endpapers **Davidson's Steam Car of 1900 with its crew of cadets.** ***Title page*** **A Chieftain tank on exercise in Germany.** ***Facing page*** **A French Renault FT two-man tank in difficulties.**

A QUARTO BOOK

Published in the United Kingdom
by New Burlington Books Ltd, London W1

This book was designed and produced by Quarto Publishing Limited, 32 Kingly Court, London W1.

Phototypeset in England by Filmtype Services Limited, Scarborough
Colour separation by Sakai Lithocolour Company Limited, Hong Kong
Printed by Leefung-Asco Printers Limited, Hong Kong

CONTENTS

THE EARLY YEARS	7
THE FIRST WORLD WAR	17
THE INTER-WAR YEARS	25
THE SECOND WORLD WAR	37
THE POST-WAR YEARS	55

Below **F. R. Simms demonstrates his Quadricycle Maxim Gun Carrier at Roehampton in 1898.** ***Top right*** **The traction engine of Fowler's Armoured Road Train sent to South Africa in 1902.** ***Bottom right*** **A contemporary drawing of the Boydell engine with its 'footed wheel'.**

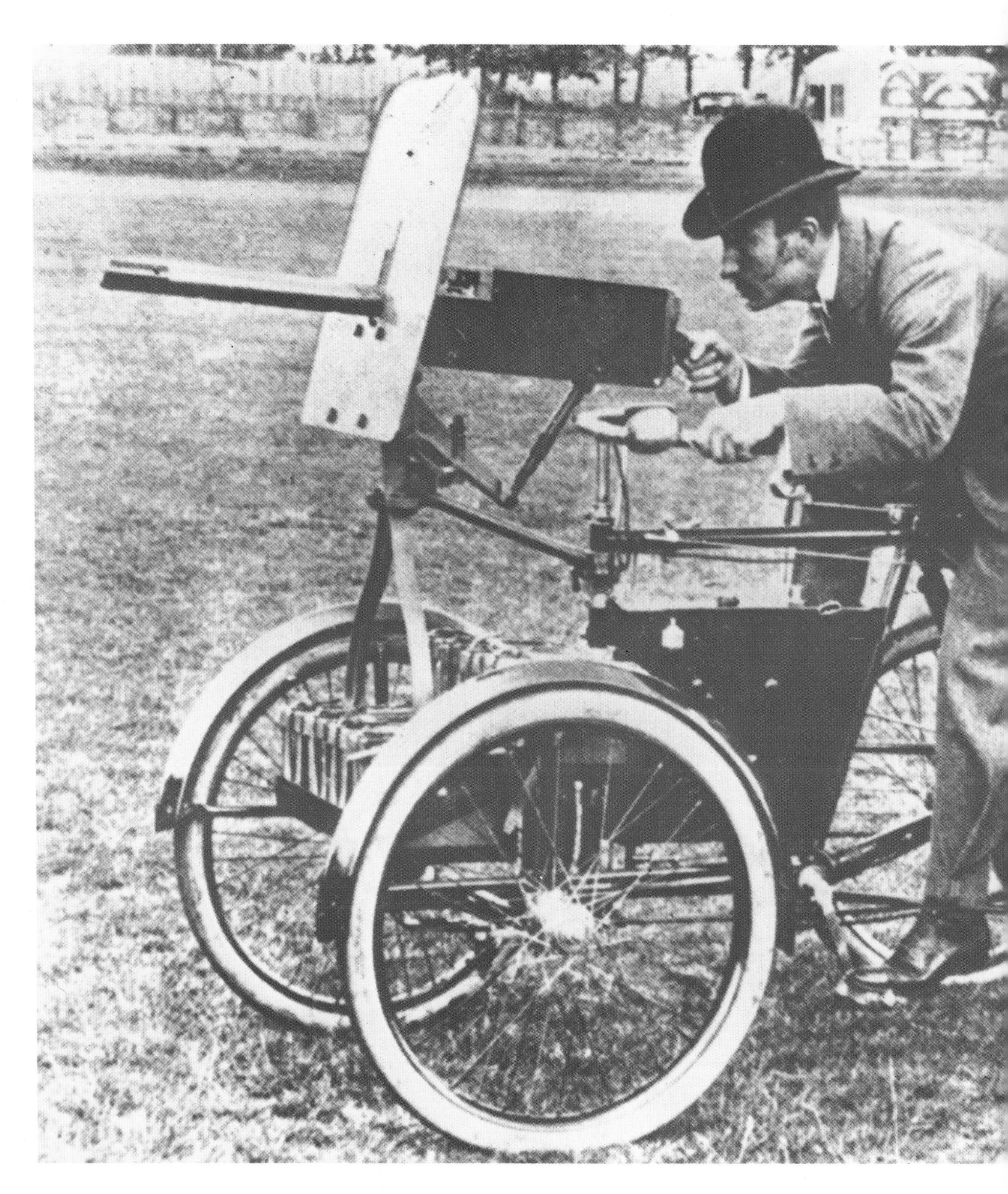

THE EARLY YEARS

IN THE 1890s, military transportation was still largely dependent upon the horse, and the vocabulary of stores of any army was replete with such descriptions as 'Wheels, Second Class, "C" No. 35', or 'Whips, Driving', or 'Carts, Forage', or 'Wagons Bread and Meat' or even 'Traces Harness, Machine Gun Nearside'. Nevertheless, mechanical traction was beginning to make itself felt in military circles, a wedge which had been slowly making its way into position for almost 50 years and which was to be hammered home with dramatic speed in the first two decades of the coming century.

During the Crimean War the difficulty of hauling supplies through the mud-wallows which passed as roads in the theatre of war led the British War Office to purchase a steam traction engine and send it out to the Crimea. The engine selected was a Boydell, using a peculiar 'footed wheel' which had performed well on ploughland in agricultural use and was expected to overcome the mud problem. The footed wheel was a wheel which had large, flat wooden blocks pivoted to its circumference, and these blocks distributed the weight of the wheel over a greater area of ground and prevented the engine from sinking in soft going. Whilst reasonably successful on farmland, it proved rather less adequate in the liquid mud of the Crimea; while the engine itself was able to proceed, the train of wagons it was supposed to draw was not provided with the footed wheel and thus sank up to the axles and proved too much of a burden for the engine to move. While this problem was being debated the campaign came to an end and the Boydell engine was shipped back to England and disposed of.

In 1858 the Royal Artillery obtained a Bray steam engine, an eight-tonner, which they tested as a possible gun-towing machine. Various tests were carried out, towing as many as three 68-pounder guns plus a number of wagons, and the testing committee reported that 'when more perfectly constructed the engine may be suitable for use in India' and that 'the engine should be employed in the Royal Arsenal in order to gain useful experience for improved construction of such engines'.

The Franco-Prussian War of 1870 brought home to Europeans (Americans had already learned the lesson during the Civil War) that railways had become a vital factor in modern military strategy

and that mobility of an army could be vastly enhanced by intelligent use of them. The German Army's triumphant advance had been facilitated by their ability to mobilize rapidly and concentrate troops by means of railway lines, and the French defence had been equally aided by the movement of bodies of troops by rail. When the German Army flowed across northern France towards Paris, the supply trains began to feel the strain once the advance moved away from convenient railways, and the Siege of Paris was conditioned by the problem of supplying the siege batteries with ammunition all the way from Germany by means of convoys of horsed wagons. The German Army bought two Fowler steam ploughing engines in England and sent them to the supply columns in France; they were not the ideal machines for the task, being of 20 tons weight and burdened with their ploughing attachments, but they performed some useful work. One notable feat was the removal of a railway engine and tender from Nanteuil to Trilport to avoid a blown-up tunnel and an uncompleted bridge, and thus place some motive power on to an engine-less length of railway line. More usually the engines were used to draw trains of wagons on the roads, loaded with ammunition, forage and other stores, from railheads to field distribution points.

The Germans' success with these vehicles seems to have been the incentive which led other armies to look at mechanical traction. In 1873 the Italians began buying steam road engines, and within three years they had 60 in use; but in 1883 they abandoned them entirely, claiming that they were too complicated, demanding too highly skilled men, who were not readily available in the Army, and were too much of a repair burden. In

TECHNOLOGY AHEAD OF ITS TIME

The fifteenth century was as much preoccupied with warfare as our own, and its greatest creative genius did not hesitate to turn his inventiveness to the technology of destruction. The siege, the defence of city or castle, provided the typical military problems. Here, Leonardo devised strategies such as diverting rivers, to defend Venice, or flood Pisa. His speculations went well outside conventional bounds. The flails of the scythed car *below* are turned by a system of gears. The armoured car *bottom* was well ahead of its time. Driven by hand or horse it had a covering of heavy wooden beams and a gap at the top for firing.

Top left **Davidson-Duryea three-wheeled car with Colt machine-gun.** ***Bottom*** **Davidson's Steam Car of 1900 with its crew of cadets.**

THE GUN MEETS THE PETROL ENGINE

When the French manufacturers of steam carriages De Dion and Bouton began to experiment with petrol engines Simms followed their progress with interest. In 1899 they produced an engine-driven quadricycle which Simms felt had potential for conversion to military purposes. He welded a tripod to the forward section of the frame so that a Maxim machine- gun could be mounted. Ammunition for the gun was held in a tray beneath the tripod.
The photograph below probably pulled in the crowds but in practice the manoeuvrability of the vehicle must have left a lot to be desired.

Simms Quadricycle without and with Maxim Gun.

1875 the French bought two Aveling engines from England and began experiments in towing artillery. In 1876 the Russians bought an Aveling and a Fowler and found them so good that they bought ten more – make unspecified – and put them to good use in the Russo-Turkish War of 1878, among other things using them to bring up the siege artillery in front of Plevna.

From then on the use of steam engines proliferated throughout Europe and it would be repetitious to detail all the trials and demonstrations recorded in military journals of the period. The first major use in war came with the British Army in South Africa in 1899; 15 engines were sent out for traction purposes, followed shortly by two ploughing engines complete with ploughs, intended to be used for the rapid throwing up of breastworks. This latter task was one which always went down well at demonstrations, but there seems to be no record of it ever being done in earnest; when breastworks are needed, it is not usually possible (or advisable) to wait for a steam engine to make its leisurely way to the position.

But before the South African War had begun there were signs that the steam traction engine might have a rival. The internal combustion engine had made an appearance and in 1896 the French Army had used some Jourdan 'oil motor engines' in the annual manoeuvres. In 1898 the Austrian Army employed motor tractors to tow artillery in hilly country during their annual exercises, and in the same year Mr. F. R. Simms, a well-known English motoring enthusiast, brought about the first combination of the petrol engine and military firepower when he demonstrated his Simms Quadricycle at Roehampton (see box above).

The Simms machine was widely publicized and appears to have spurred others on to design 'war cars' of one sort or another. Later in 1898 Major R. P. Davidson, commandant of the North-western Military and Naval Academy at Lake Geneva, Wisconsin (not, in spite of its title, an official establishment but one of many private 'military' schools commonplace at that time in the USA) designed a three-wheeled car which was built by the Charles P. Duryea Company of Peoria. This vehicle mounted an M1895 Colt 'Potato-Digger' machine gun

Left Simms' War Car of 1902 showing the shaped protective plating and two Maxim guns. _Upper right_ The Charron Girardot et Voight armoured gun carrier of 1900 with the gun in open barbette. _Lower right_ The Erhardt anti-balloon gun of 1909. _Bottom right_ The Charron Girardot et Voight armoured car built for the Russian Army.

over the front wheels in a similar manner to Simms' design, but it was large enough to accommodate a three-man machine gun crew in addition to the driver. The gun could be operated while the vehicle was moving and, on arrival at its destination, the crew could dismount with the gun and go into action while the car returned to cover. The Davidson idea of divorcing the firepower task from the transportation function produced a more practical idea – or would have done had the vehicle been more reliable. Contemporary accounts suggest that Davidson and his cadets spent more time mending the car than driving it, and in the following year he had it rebuilt into a four-wheeler, which proved more reliable. He then designed a steam-powered car along the same lines and had two of these built in the Academy workshop in 1900, using them for some years thereafter in cadet manoeuvres. But no official interest was roused.

In 1900 also, a steam car was built in Russia; little is known of it except that it was built by an engineer named Lutski to the orders of the Imperial Artillery Commission, and it is probable that it was primarily intended as a gun tractor. In any event, trials showed that, like most steam vehicles, it was overweight and underpowered, and the experiment was abandoned.

By this time the automobile was no longer a curiosity, especially in France, and the French Army were probably the first to adopt motor cars for transportation of staff officers. Fired by this military interest, Charron Girardot et Voight, makers of the successful CGV racing cars, constructed an armoured gun carrier by placing an armoured barbette or tonneau at the rear of a touring car chassis and providing it with a Hotchkiss machine gun. Two men manned the gun, a driver controlled the vehicle and an officer supervised. The Army bought the car and, after using it in the 1901 exercises, sent it to Morocco, where it vanished into obscurity.

The early years of the century saw the motor vehicle adopted in increasing numbers as a commercial carrier as motor lorries increased in numbers and armies slowly began to purchase them. They were not cheap, however, and the prospect of financing a full-scale re-equipping with motor trucks could not be contemplated. For many years, though, there had been a variety of subsidy schemes, whereby horse owners promised to furnish horses to the army in the event of mobilization in return for an annual retainer, and this system was extended to motor vehicles. The Germans appear to have originated this, introducing a system under which commercial operators of trucks could receive a grant of £150 to assist in the purchase of the vehicle, followed by an annual subsidy of £60 per annum for four years. The condition was that if, during the subsidy period, the army mobilized, then the truck was taken for military use. If no mobilization occurred, then the operator was in pocket and, presumably, receptive to the suggestion that he might buy another on the same terms. By the beginning of 1914 the German Army had 825 such subsidized trucks available to it and, together with wholly-owned military trucks, could provide five transport columns each of 10 vehicles for each of the 25 regular Army

Corps. (*Jahrbuch für Deutsche Armee und Marine,* February 1914.) In the same month the *Kriegstechnische Zeitschrift* announced that there were 3,213 motor tractors of 10–40hp and 513 of over 40hp available to be requisitioned in Germany in the event of war, and a 1913 census showed 7,700 heavy trucks and 50,000 cars and light trucks in use in Germany.

Unfortunately, few of these vehicles were of much use away from a surfaced road; the narrow high-pressure tyres of the day were useless on soft ground. This was highlighted by a 1913 report that the Italian Army had adapted a motor tractor for their new 15cm howitzer, but only for road movement; a team of horses accompanied the howitzer and took over the haulage once the road was left behind.

While the commercial vehicle had been gaining ground, one or two suggestions had appeared for more specifically military designs and, particularly, designs incorporating armour protection. As early as 1896 a Mr. E. J. Pennington proposed a war car which was to use a four-wheeled chassis surmounted by a 'bathtub' armoured body above which stood two shielded Maxim guns on pedestal mounts. This idea got no further than the drawing board, but in 1902 F. R. Simms appeared once again with a vehicle resembling the Pennington design, having the same 'bathtub' superstructure open at the top with guns on pedestal mountings. Five men operated this vehicle; one in the centre drove it, two manned a Maxim one-pounder 'pom-pom' at one end of the body, and two others each manned a Maxim machine gun at the other end. Protected by 6.3mm (¼-in) armour, Simms' War Car weighed 6½ tons, was 8.5m (28ft) long and could move at 14km/hr (9mph). But in spite of demonstrating the car at various motor shows in 1902-3, Simms could raise no interest in the design and he eventually scrapped it.

The Russian Army, having had no success with Engineer Lutski, now called upon the French firm of Charron Girardot et Voight to inspect its armoured gun carrier, but turned it down. The Russian General Staff then laid down a brief specification, indicating what they thought was desirable, passed it to Charron Girardot et Voight, and asked for 36 armoured cars to be made. The resulting vehicle might be said to be the prototype of all the armoured cars which followed; it was a four-wheeled boxy

structure of armour plate surmounted by a revolving turret on the roof in which was mounted a Maxim machine gun, its water-jacket protected by an armoured trough. Steel channel-section girders were strapped along the sides, from where they could be quickly removed and thrown across a ditch to allow the vehicle to pass across. Weighing just over three tons and driven by a 30bhp engine, the Charron was a practical vehicle; the first was delivered to Russia in 1904 and was used for riot control in St. Petersburg, but for some unknown reason the Russians now repudiated the contract and refused to take more. The second car, already built, was bought by the French Army, and no further cars were made.

Probably stimulated by reports of the Charron car, the Austro-Daimler company began looking at armoured car design in late 1903. Their design was of the same general form, a high-set bonnet concealing the engine, with a square cab for the driver and a box body with revolving turret on top, mounting a Skoda machine gun. The driver could see through slits in the armour or, when conditions allowed, could elevate his seat so as to raise his head through a hatch on the cab top, allowing him all-round vision. The Austro-Daimler weighed some 3½ tons, could move at 45km/hr (28mph), and was used by the Imperial Army in the 1905 and 1906 manoeuvres with some success, though no more were bought.

During the next few years one or two other armoured car designs appeared, all of which followed the Charron design. But at this same time a new problem was presenting itself to the military – the heavier-than-air machine and the airship. Both these had reached a point in their development where they were being contemplated for military use, primarily as reconnaissance machines, and the question of air defence arose. The question had, in fact, arisen before; in 1870 the French used balloons to escape from besieged Paris and the German Army had produced a number of 25mm rifles mounted on light carts, the idea being that several equipages were dispersed around the perimeter of Paris and as soon as a balloon was seen ascending the guns turned out like a fire brigade and rushed to intercept its flight. The same principle was now applied using motor vehicles. In 1909, at

Left **The Austro-Daimler car of 1903 with the driver raised so as to have better vision when not in combat.** ***This page top right*** **An armoured machine-gun carrier, designed by the Hotchkiss company, which offered little protection to the driver.** ***Bottom*** **The Rheinmetall anti-balloon gun of 1909 in a 'half-armoured car'.**

the Frankfurt International Exhibition, the two major gunmakers of Germany, Krupp and the Rheinische Metalwaren und Maschinenfabrik (who later adopted the shorter form Rheinmetall by which they are still known), both showed 'motor balloon guns'. In the Krupp design a 75mm gun was mounted on the rear of a 50hp truck, capable of a speed of 45km/hr (28mph). Krupp's greatest problem was to reduce the recoil blow on the chassis when the gun was fired, and this was done by an ingenious system known as differential recoil. Briefly, what happened was that the gun was pulled back against its recoil springs, held back, and loaded; it was then released, to run forward in its mounting, propelled by the spring. A fraction of a second before it reached the fully-forward position, the gun was fired, so that the recoil force had first to arrest the moving mass, then reverse it. This reduced the recoil blow to about one-quarter of its normal force, bringing it within the capability of the chassis to sustain it.

The Rheinmetall design was a 50mm gun mounted in a turret on an armoured car. A contemporary report described it as follows: 'To protect the car, its equipment and gun detachment from hostile fire it is armoured throughout, including the

wheels, with 3mm of nickel steel. The entrance, the peep-hole for the driver, and the embrasures in the sides can all be closed and the forward part of the car shut down. The gun with its armoured turret can be revolved on a turntable, and the embrasures are provided with shutters.' There was some debate as to the virtue of armour in this context; it seemed unlikely that the gun would be under fire from the balloon or airship at which it was firing, and there seemed little likelihood of it operating so far forward as to come under fire. An alternative reason advanced was that the addition of the armour was simply there to add weight and make the vehicle more sturdy to absorb the recoil of the 5cm gun without having to indulge in Krupp's differential recoil solution.

Whatever the truth of the matter,

THE INVENTORS

The main enthusiasm of Mr. F. R. Simms *top left* was motoring, but this led him to the first combination of petrol engine and military firepower. He may have inspired Davidson *top right* to design his three-wheeled car mounting a detachable machine-gun. It was Swinton *bottom left* who saw the need for armoured tracked vehicles, and it was his persuasion which worked on responsible bodies such as the Landships Committee. Wilson *bottom right* designed the transmission for early tanks. His improved versions were on all British WWII tanks.

Rheinmetall also displayed a half-armoured car mounting the same 5cm gun. This resembled an ordinary touring car with the gun mounted on a pedestal behind the driver. This reduced the weight by a considerable amount, though without requiring any modification to the recoil system. Strictly speaking these vehicles represent the earliest attempts at self-propelled guns rather than armoured cars, but they were of considerable interest at the time and they demonstrated that it was possible to mount something heavier than a machine gun on to a motor chassis and get away with it.

But for all the clever designs, the soldiers were highly resistant. In 1905 the US Chief of Staff General Miles proposed converting five cavalry regiments to armoured cars, a suggestion which upset the horsemen and caused such violent opposition that it was eventually abandoned. Having just upset the Ordnance Department by suggesting that their sea-coast gun carriage designs were obsolete by European standards, Miles had thus alienated about half the US Army, and after that he was more careful in the ideas he advanced. At much the same time the Russian Army had used some motor cars in manoeuvres, and the complaint was heard that the 'noise and smell were intolerable' and that horses refused to pass the vehicles.

The most telling point in favour of the horse was, of course, that the motor vehicle was still only useful on a surfaced road, and by the end of the first decade of the century this disadvantage was sufficiently marked to cause a number of inventors to look into ways of making the motor into a cross-country vehicle. It will be recalled that the Boydell engine used in the Crimean War had a footed wheel, which spread the weight on soft ground, though not well enough, and there had been a number of improvements and variations on that theme. In 1886 the Applegarth tractor had been patented, a steam tractor which used an endless track around its wheel and which extended forward to an idler out of contact with the ground. One advantage of this design was that it allowed the machine to clamber across uneven ground. A more practical design was the Batter tractor of 1888, patented in the USA. This used endless tracks in long contact with the ground, and was driven by two steam engines, one driving each track.

In 1908 the Hornsby company of Grantham developed a tracked tractor in which an oil engine drove a sprocket which propelled an endless track, giving excellent cross-country performance. Hornsby's demonstrated this at the Royal Review in 1908, and in the following year they entered the machine in a War Office trial for cross-country tractors, which it won handsomely, collecting the first prize of £1,000 plus a bonus of £180 for 'general excellence'. But that was as far as it went, and no orders came in to Hornsby's factory. In the end, in order to

Below **The Hornsby-Ackroyd tractor of 1907 which successfully competed in the War Office trials but did not win any military orders.**

recoup some of their development costs, Hornsby's sold their patented track system to an American company, the Holt Tractor Company of Stockton, California. In the Western states of America there was plenty of scope for the caterpillar tractor (as it had come to be known) and within a short time Holt's were busy producing 70hp and 45hp tractors for sale throughout the USA and then in Europe.

In 1911 a young Austrian officer, Lieutenant Gunther Burstyn, saw a Holt tractor at work; he was already familiar with armoured cars and their limitations, and he saw in the Holt track a method of overcoming the armoured car's cross-country problem. He set about designing a suitable vehicle, and in October 1911 submitted drawings to the Austro-Hungarian War Department.

After three months' deliberation, they returned the drawings; a clever idea, they said, and the young officer was to be commended upon his ingenuity. Would he, perhaps, be kind enough to build one so that the idea could be tested? At his own expense, of course. Not having that kind of money, Burstyn could not build one, nor could he interest a commercial manufacturer in the idea; he sent his drawings to the German War Department, which turned the idea down. He then tried to patent it, but this was refused on the grounds that the vehicle was driven by a petrol engine and this method of propulsion had already been patented, while the rest of his design was too impractical to be worth patenting. Disillusioned, Burstyn abandoned his design; he later turned up with another brilliant idea, a short-barrelled muzzle-loading mortar which could be used to fire small bombs out of trenches. They didn't think much of that one either.

At much the same time, across the world, a young Australian civil engineer, L. A. de Mole, was faced with the problem of moving heavy loads across rough country, and he designed a tracked vehicle for the task. Having done so, he was struck by the possibility of military applications of the design and sent drawings to the War Office in London in 1912. They were returned, with a letter stating that the War Office was not interested in experimenting with 'chain rail machines'. De Mole's design was of considerable interest, since he suggested steering it by 'bowing' the tracks; the suspension wheels were mounted on pivoted sub-assemblies at each end of the tracks, while the whole assembly had sufficient play to allow the pivoting unit to pull the track round into a bend, round which the vehicle would steer. It was several years before this idea appeared again.

Below **An early tank, painted in disruptive camouflage and stowing the unditching beam and rails on the roof.** ***Right*** **Lanchester armoured cars in Belgium, 1915.**

The First World War

In spite of several inventors attempting to interest various military authorities in different types of cross-country machines, when war broke out in 1914 the armies involved had little to show except a scattering of commercial trucks and motor cars and a handful of prototype armoured cars, most of which were, by that time, somewhat elderly. The first few months of war called for little revision of this situation; the horsed troops performed as they had always done and mobility appeared satisfactory. The motor vehicle made some impact in the famous 'Taxis of the Marne' incident, when the Paris taxis were commandeered to rush troops out to stem the German advance on the city, but this, obviously, was an unusual event; had more notice been given, then the poilus would have marched in the traditional and normal fashion – and probably would have arrived too tired to fight. But at the end of 1914, when the 'race to the sea' was run and the trench lines ran from the Channel to the Alps, things began to take on a different hue.

Upon the outbreak of war, of course, the various subsidy schemes had been called due; this brought about 1,000 trucks into the British Army, probably twice that number to the French and an estimated 30,000 vehicles of all kinds to the German Army, though this figure was made up of subsidy vehicles and outright impressment. Once the war settled into a siege operation these trucks began to demonstrate the advantages of mechanical over horsed traction, and all the combatant armies began increasing their holdings as fast as they could. For Germany and Austria this meant building, while Britain and France not only built but were also able to purchase from America. Not only the numbers but also the types of vehicle expanded beyond pre-war comprehension; most armies had, in the hope of standardization, classified vehicles into broad groups – passenger cars, light trucks (to 1½ ton) and heavy trucks (3 ton). But this neat division was soon shattered by, firstly, the influx of civilian vehicles, which did not fit neatly into these groups, and secondly the sudden demand for specialized vehicles – petrol tankers, ambulances, gun carriages, gun tractors, field kitchens, mobile dental surgeries, searchlight carriers, workshop trucks and innumerable others – of which some were variations on existing vehicles while others were new from the wheels up.

While the soft-skinned vehicles began to proliferate, there was also a rise in the armoured car field. The first armoured cars to see action were a number of Minerva and SAVA touring cars, which Belgian officers had sheathed in boiler-plate, mounted Maxim guns, and used to hold up the advance of the German

cavalry units with some success. Late in August 1914 a Royal Naval Air Service squadron was sent to Ostend in order to assist the operations of the Naval Brigade, and with it went 18 assorted motor cars, primarily intended to go out and rescue aviators who had to make forced landings. Some of these landings were uncomfortably close to the enemy, and after one or two incidents where the cars came under fire from forward German troops, two of the cars were given boiler-plate protection. In September Mr. Winston Churchill authorized the provision of a hundred cars fitted with machine guns, and, after some experiments with boiler plate armouring on the spot, it was decided to build proper armoured bodies on to the chassis in Britain. Rolls-Royce, Lanchester, Talbot and Delaunay-Belleville car chassis were obtained and a more-or-less standard form of body devised. The bonnet and driver's compartment were protected by steel plate, and a revolving turret carrying a Maxim gun was mounted on the roof. The rear section of the chassis was left as a flat-bed truck so that loads could be carried. In addition to these, a number of Seabrook trucks were armoured and fitted with obsolescent three-pounder Hotchkiss guns from naval stocks and with Maxim machine guns; the intention here

was that these trucks, with a crew of nine or ten men, could be rushed out to give support to the armoured cars when opposition became too great for a single car.

Whilst satisfactory, these cars had a short life in their intended role, since once the war settled down to its static phase their opportunities for action became less and less. Eventually the armoured car squadrons were withdrawn from France and sent to other theatres, where they could be of more use – two went to Gallipoli but were of little use there, others went to German South West Africa, Mesopotamia, and one even to Russia and Lapland.

As the trench lines proliferated and barbed wire grew thickly between them, and as the machine gun began to dominate the front line, several people began to ponder the problem of breaking through this formidable obstacle, and inevitably they began to think about mechanical methods of doing it.

Leaving aside the numerous inventors who suggested shields on wheels, modified steam-rollers and similar devices simply to push down the wire, the first man to put a foot on the right track was Lieutenant-Colonel (later Major-General Sir) Ernest Swinton of the Royal Engineers. Swinton was a professional soldier who had fought in South Africa, edited the official *History of the Russo-Japanese War*, served as secretary of the Committee of Imperial Defence and written several books (one of which, *The Defence of Duffer's Drift*, became a minor classic and the standard textbook on small-unit tactics for the next 50 years). At the outbreak of war he had been sent to France as the official war correspondent; the army of 1914 was not keen to have ordinary civilian reporters wandering around in the combat zone and asking awkward questions, so Swinton, under the alias of 'Eyewitness', provided all the newspapers with material. (This system lasted until the middle of 1915, after which reporters were authorized and Swinton moved to other duties.) On 19 October 1914, Swinton was returning to England for a conference and, *en route*, was pondering the problem of enabling troops to advance in the face of wire and machine guns. What was required, he concludes, was 'a power-driven, bullet-proof, armed engine capable of destroying machine guns, of crossing country and trenches, of breaking through entanglements and of climbing earthworks'. And while thinking about this, he remembered a letter he had received in July, before war broke out, from a South African engineer called Marriott, drawing his attention to the Holt tractor and suggesting that such a tracked vehicle might have applications for military transport. At the time Swinton had passed the idea to the Transportation Department in the War Office and thought no more about it, but he now saw that the tracked tractor offered a basis for the cross-country vehicle which he envisaged.

Upon arriving in London Swinton put his idea to Sir Maurice Hankey, then Sec-

Facing page, above **The Holt tractor, as used for towing artillery, 1915.** ***Facing page, below*** **One example of the many types of improvised armoured cars used in Belgium in 1914/15.** ***Below*** **French 'Artillerie d'Assault' in action near Soissons, July 1918.**

retary of the Committee of Imperial Defence. Hankey saw merit in the idea and suggested Swinton should put the proposition to Lord Kitchener, then Secretary of State for War. Kitchener, however, was too busy to see Swinton, who returned to France, but a few days later Hankey saw Kitchener and broached Swinton's idea. Predictably, Kitchener would have none of it.

Hankey now turned in another direction; in addition to his post with the Committee of Imperial Defence, he was secretary to the War Council, and his terms of reference there gave him the duty to place before the council and the Prime Minister any matters which he felt to be of importance to the war effort.

Accordingly, over Christmas 1914 Hankey wrote a memorandum for the Prime Minister, Mr. Asquith. After expounding on conditions in France and the problems facing the army, he went on to suggest 'numbers of large heavy rollers, themselves bullet-proof, propelled from behind by motor-engines geared very low, the driving wheel fitted with caterpillar driving gear to grip the ground, the driver's seat armoured, and with a Maxim gun fitted...' Mr. Asquith circulated Hankey's paper among the War Council; one of the members was the First Lord of the Admiralty, Mr. Winston Churchill, a gentleman who was always anxious to keep the Royal Navy in the forefront of developments and contributing to the war effort in any conceivable way.

Churchill had already been giving this matter some thought and had instigated some investigations into trench-crossing devices; fired by Hankey's paper he produced a memorandum of his own, expounding and expanding on Hankey, and he followed this up by setting up an Admiralty Landships Committee to investigate the problem and prepare designs of vehicle. This committee proposed numerous devices and tested others

THE MOTORCYCLE AT WAR

The 1914/18 War gave a great impetus to the motorcycle. It was used for despatch-carrying (*top left* a BSA in German East Africa), as a machine-gun carrier (*top right* the 24th Motor M.G. Battalion, June 1918; *below* the Vickers-Clyno machine-gun combination) and female auxiliaries ferried staff officers (*bottom*) in motorcycle combinations.

over the next six months or so. Meanwhile Swinton, in France and quite unaware of the Landships Committee's existence or activities, refined his original idea and sent another memorandum, complete with specifications of a possible machine and some ideas on how to use it, to Sir John French, C-in-C of the British Army in France. Sir John forwarded it to the War Office, where it appears to have finally stimulated some sort of response; a week later, at the end of June 1915, the War Office sent a representative to sit on the Landships Committee.

Shortly after this Swinton returned from France to take up an appointment as Secretary of the Dardanelles Committee of the War Cabinet, a post which gave him sufficient authority to ask questions wherever he liked, and he soon discovered that not only was there the Landships Committee but several other minor agencies all beavering away at the same problem. Late in August 1915, having obtained the backing of the Prime Minister, Swinton managed to get all these people into the same room together to discuss what they were doing and how they were going about it. As a result, it was agreed that since the Admiralty appeared to have the best-working organization, they could continue to develop the machine, but that the War Office would say what the specification should be and the Ministry of Munitions would give any assistance needed in the supply of material and equipment and, once the design was perfected, take over the production. One advantage of this system was that for the first time the people concerned with the design of the vehicle were given some facts and figures about what sort of obstacles the machine would have to overcome.

Bottom left **A Whippet tank, photographed behind the German lines at Morcourt in 1918.** ***Top*** **Little Willie as it is today, in the Tank Museum, Bovington.** ***Bottom*** **Little Willie as it was, undergoing its early trials in 1916.**

At this time some experimental work was being done at the Lincoln factory of William Foster & Sons, a firm of agricultural engineers well known for their tractors. Foster's director, Sir William Tritton, working with Lieutenant Wilson, a naval armoured car expert, had moved away from the various devices the Landships Committee had called for and his firm had designed a machine of their own, known variously as the Wilson, the Tritton or the Lincoln No. 1 machine. This was little more than a steel box mounted upon a lengthened Holt tractor track unit. It was proposed to fit it with a rotating turret on top, but this was felt to add too much complication to the construction and the idea was dropped. Eventually, on 10 September 1915, the Tritton machine was tried out, but the results were

inauspicious; the track had a poor grip, tended to come off its guide wheels, and, due to its position, gave little obstacle-crossing performance. The track and its suspension were entirely redesigned and the new version, known as Little Willie, ran successfully in December 1915.

In order to meet the War Office requirement that the machine should be able to climb a 1.2m (4ft) parapet and cross a 2.4m (8ft) trench, Wilson set about redesigning the layout of the track. One of the earliest ideas to come before the Landships Committee had been a Big Wheel Machine, which was to use wheels of 12m (40ft) diameter so as to overcome obstacles – a figure arrived at by careful mathematical analysis of German trench parapet widths. Such a device was hopelessly impractical, but Wilson fastened on to the 12m (40ft) wheel and reasoned that if he shaped the front of the vehicle's hull to approximate to a segment of such a wheel, and then ran the track around it, he would arrive at a 'wheel' of the requisite diameter without actually being encumbered by the rest of it. And in this fashion the shape of the first armoured fighting tracked vehicle was arrived at.

The first tank – though that name had not yet been coined in this context – took shape as a rhomboidal steel casing with sponsons on each side, armed with ex-naval six-pounder guns, and with ports through which another five machine guns could be fired by the crew. The machine was propelled by a Daimler engine, sitting in the centre of the one and only compartment, driving via a two-speed-and-reverse gearbox to a large differential, from which cross-shafts ran to the sides of the tank to sliding pinion gears giving another two-speed range. From here the drive went by heavy chains to the track driving sprockets at the rear of the tank. The driver sat high in the front, controlling the tank by means of a throttle, with a gear lever controlling the primary gearbox; two 'gearsmen' operated the secondary two-speed gears on the cross-shaft, acting on hand signals from the driver. As might be imagined, to co-ordinate a successful gear change was a matter demanding considerable practice and no small amount of luck.

The first of these machines was called the Centipede, Foster's registered trade name for their agricultural tractors; this was all very well for restricted use among those 'in the know', but in the interest of secrecy some innocuous cover name was needed. Several expedient tales had already been told to the factory hands engaged in making the machine: the mechanical components were said to be for a Demonstration and Instructional Chassis for some unspecified military driving school, while the hull plating was said to be for 'special water carriers for use in Mesopotamia'. This latter explanation led to the workforce referring to it as 'that tank thing'. This must have stayed in the mind of Colonel Swinton as, on Christmas Eve 1915, he sat with a companion, Lieut.-Colonel Dally Jones, to draw up a report on the progress of Centipede. One of the questions under review was the matter of a cover name, and after considering and rejecting several suggestions they finally settled on the word tank to describe the new machine. It is extremely doubtful if either of them ever contemplated the repercussions of their decision and the extent to which the word would enter the language of the world.

On 12 January 1916, the first tank moved under its own power; on 28 January it arrived, under conditions of great secrecy, at Hatfield in Hertfordshire, was unloaded under cover of darkness and driven under heavy escort to Hatfield Park, where it was to be demonstrated to various high-ranking figures in military and political circles. On 29 January it made a preliminary canter around a course of obstacles, constructed to give as realistic a picture of front line conditions as possible, and on 2 February the official unveiling took place, when

THE MOTHERS OF THEM ALL

The original British tanks, showing their evolution and improvement in the war years. *Below* The original Mark I, with tail steering gear. *Below left* The Mark II 'Female' with machine-gun in place of 6-pounder in the sponson. *Below right* A Mark IV from the rear quarter. *Top right* A Mark V showing the improved type of sponson with 6-pounder and machine-gun. *Centre right* The Mark VIII 'Liberty' tank, built by Britain and the USA. *Bottom right* The supply tank Mark IX which could carry reserve troops and stores to accompany an attack.

Below left **A Renault FT17 tank in Bovington Museum.**
Below right **Holt tractors towing 8 inch howitzers in France, 1918.**
Bottom **The American six-ton tank M1918, based on the Renault FT design.**

Mother, as the tank came to be called, performed in the hands of Chief Petty Officer Hill of the Royal Naval Air Service, the first man in history to be known as a tank driver. The display, witnessed by Lloyd George, Minister of Munitions, General Sir William Robertson, Chief of the Imperial General Staff, Lord Kitchener and other luminaries, was a success and eight days later the first order was given for the construction of tanks for military use.

We have dwelt at some length on the genesis of the first tank, since it was a most significant step in the development of military transport, but it should be pointed out that similar developments were taking place in other countries at much the same time. In France there were many suggestions for armoured rollers and similar devices and, as in Britain, the impetus came from consideration of the Holt tractor. The Schneider company were agents for the Holt, selling their tractors to the French Army as gun-towing vehicles, and in June 1915 they began contemplating adding armour and weapons to turn the Holt into a fighting machine. The

result was demonstrated in December 1915, and in the same month, quite independently, a Colonel Estienne, having seen some Holt tractors towing guns, wrote to General Joffre suggesting a Holt-based armoured vehicle. On Joffre's authority, Estienne visited the Renault company with his ideas, but Louis Renault was reluctant to get involved. Estienne then went to Schneider, discovered that they were already working on the lines he proposed, and Estienne, together with Brillie, the Schneider engineer, drew up a detailed design based on Brillie's mechanical knowledge and Estienne's knowledge of what the vehicle might be called upon to do. The result was the Schneider CA tank, which went into production in late September 1916.

Unfortunately Estienne had upset several people by his short-cut approach via General Joffre; the official *Service Technical d'Automobile* felt that their function had been usurped, and that they

had, therefore, better get ahead and develop an official design to put Estienne in his place. This resulted in the Saint Chamond tank, which was far from as successful as its designers hoped. In the end, the French became somewhat disillusioned with heavy tanks and opted instead to go for light, fast, two-man tanks which would 'swarm' over the battlefield in the spirit of '*attaque à l'outrance*', a policy which resulted in the Renault FT.

The German Army was surprised and shaken by the appearance of the first tanks, but they were reluctant to consider adopting such devices themselves; the first British use of tanks, in unsuitable ground, led to large numbers being bogged down in mud, and this led the Germans to the opinion that they were of little practical value once the novelty had worn off. They were as slow as the British and French to see that success with tanks was a question of applying them in substantial force on suitable terrain. There was also the stated policy of the German High Command that they would 'not fight a battle of *matériel*' but would rely upon superior manpower to crush the enemy. This opinion was eventually overturned and the German Army began the development of tank designs of their own, but it was left so late that no more than a handful had been made before the Armistice, and the major part of German tank strength was made up of captured Allied machines.

Below **A Schneider-Citroën-Kegresse half-track car of 1923, armed with a 37mm gun.**
Facing page **The French 75mm 'Auto-Cannon', an anti-aircraft gun on a De Dion Bouton chassis.**

THE INTER WAR YEARS

THERE IS A NATURAL TENDENCY to regard the tank as being the primary mechanical innovation of the World War I, which of course it was; but this should not be allowed to conceal the enormous increase in the number of more mundane mechanically propelled vehicles which the armies adopted. As well as normal cargo-carrying trucks, used for providing every sort of supply to the front, there were increasing numbers of specialized vehicles making their appearance. The gradual rise of air power led to the emergence of the anti-aircraft gun, and, doubtless influenced by the same considerations as had led to the designs seen in Frankfurt in 1909, the idea of mounting anti-aircraft guns on to motor chassis so as to provide a highly mobile defensive force capable of rapid redeployment was one which was widely used. The French mounted their ubiquitous 75mm M1897 field gun into a high-angle mounting and placed this on the rear of a De Dion Bouton chassis to produce the Auto-cannon, while Britain followed suit and placed its 3in gun on to Thorneycroft and Peerless three-ton motor trucks. These, of course, were supplemented by trucks mounting searchlights and sound-locating equipment. The rise in the amount of complicated armament – and in the quantity of motor vehicles – led to the design of special workshop vehicles, equipped with power tools, which could be brought close to the forward areas to cope with light repairs and maintenance. In order to move field artillery more quickly, the French developed the '*portée*' system, in which a 75mm gun and its limber could be run on to the back of a four-tonne truck and rapidly driven to a new location. Taking this idea a stage further, the Schneider company began mounting heavier weapons, up to a 28cm howitzer, on to Holt-type tracked chassis, thus developing the first tracked self-propelled guns.

One drawback which still remained, however, was the inability of most wheeled vehicles to move once they left a made-up road surface, particularly in the glutinous mud which inevitably makes its

appearance close to the front line. The Russians, with a lesser proportion of hard roads than any other combatant, found this particularly restrictive, and their armoured cars were greatly hampered in their tactics. One solution was advanced by Adolphe Kegresse, a French engineer employed as the superintendent of the Czar's personal fleet of automobiles, who removed the standard rear axle, moved it forward, added a second rear axle and wheels, and then ran a flexible rubber track around both sets of wheels to turn the vehicle into a half-track. After trying the idea on some cars, it was applied to a number of Austin armoured cars with considerable success. It has been suggested, and there seems some merit in the idea, that Kegresse took his inspiration from a number of American Lombard half-track tractors, which the Russians purchased in 1916 for use as artillery prime movers. The Lombard had been invented in 1901 by Alvin Lombard of Waterville, Maine, and his original model was steam-powered and used for hauling logs out of the New England woods.

When the Revolution took place in Russia, Kegresse, doubtless because of his place of employment, wisely took to his heels and returned to France, and after the war he patented various aspects of his half-track idea and interested a number of manufacturers in it, as a result of which it was one of the most important automotive aspects of the 1920s. A convoy of Citroën-Kegresse half-tracks made a famous expedition across the Sahara, over terrain which no wheeled vehicle of the day could have traversed, and military circles began to take considerable interest. In Britain the Crossley Motor Company, which had supplied large quantities of trucks and cars to the military forces during the war, began to develop Kegresse's patents under licence, while the Burford Company also took out a licence. A similar device was developed by the Roadless Traction Company, but in their track unit the original axle of the vehicle was retained, fitted with a driving wheel, and the track unit was laid out forward of the rear axle; one advantage claimed for the Roadless system was that the track unit had a degree of lateral freedom which made steering the vehicle a great deal easier. An interesting variation was the Morris-Martel-Roadless, in which the Roadless track unit went at the front of the vehicle and the steered wheels at the back. Eventually a number of these half-track vehicles were adopted; the British used a Morris-Roadless in India for gun towing, and the French adopted a Citroën-Kegresse for the same task. Other French half-tracks included armoured cars, engineer vehicles, bridge layers, troop carriers and recovery vehicles.

Facing page top **The original Austin-Patilov Russian armoured car, converted to a half-track by Kegresse.** ***Facing page bottom*** **The British 3 inch AA gun on a Peerless lorry mounting. Numbers of these survived until World War II.** ***Below*** **The Crossley-Kegresse infantry carrier adopted by the British Army.** ***Top left*** **Martel's one-man tankette prototype.** ***Middle left*** **The Citroën-Kegresse of 1923.** ***Bottom left*** **The Austin twin-turret armoured car as supplied to Russia in 1915/16. These were later converted by Kegresse.**

This latter tabulation tends to indicate the development of specialized military vehicles in their own right, outside the normal run of commercial production, and this, of course, was becoming more and more necessary. Commercial vehicles could be utilized for simple road transport, but when it came to the various specialized tasks of a modern army, there were few commercial equivalents, and armies were being driven to designing their own and, in some cases, even building prototypes to place before manufacturers.

Whether the manufacturers would respond was a different matter; automobile-makers exist to produce profits for their shareholders, and it was increasingly obvious during the 1920s that this, could be done by settling on an easily made design and producing it in volume. Items such as half a dozen bridge carriers, two recovery trucks or a tank transporter had to be largely hand-made, away from the production line, and they absorbed more money than they produced. Nevertheless, there were sufficient manufacturers with a sense of patriotic feeling who were prepared to allow their commercial production to subsidize a proportion of their military designing; they had to, since the military – in any country in the 1920s – were starved of money.

The years between the wars, then, were years in which much fundamental research was done but which produced little mass production of specialized military vehicles. But sufficient vehicles were made, in short production runs or in ones and twos, to indicate success or failure of an idea, after which it was laid away and some new line of approach pursued. Some of the ideas were more spectacular than others, but they all contributed something.

One idea which was to have far-reaching effects, was the machine-gun carrier, and it originated in Britain. It seems to have been born out of a confusion of tactical and economic theory, and whilst the economics may have been sensible the tactical side now shows itself to have been weak and muddled. World War I had left the British Army well prepared mentally to fight the campaign of 1919, indeed in 1939 that was what it set out to do, and though there was the firm belief that there would be no more wars in Europe, there was at the same time the deeply rooted instinct that if it came then everyone would dive back into their trenches again. The machine-gun carrier was originally intended to do as its name suggests, carry a machine gun, and it was to

carry it across bullet-swept ground whilst protecting its crew from harm. Sensible enough, you might imagine, but totally at variance with the experiences of 1917 and the mud of Passchendaele, where any such vehicle would have been bogged down. However, small vehicles are cheap and there was also the cavalry-like concept of small individual armoured vehicles dashing about the battlefield, and this had its attractions for the theorists.

The first ideas were for one-man tanks. Actually they were not tanks at all, but poorly protected carriers, and the prototype was built by Major Gifford Martel at his own expense using commercial components. The War Office was sufficiently interested to give an order for four to Morris Motors, and the trials of these quickly showed up the deficiencies of the one-man idea. Meanwhile John Carden and a Mr. Loyd built a similar vehicle, but quickly moved to a two-man crew with a fully tracked suspension. The War Office liked these better and tried them in the Mechanized Force Tests of 1928-9. This was enough for Vickers, who bought out Carden-Loyd and marketed the little carriers themselves, pointing out to their customers that the British Army was using them. The development continued and the suspension was greatly improved, though it was never capable of carrying heavy loads nor of travelling at high speeds. It was recognizable by the fact that the roadwheels were small rollers pinned to an external frame outside the hull and carrying the idler wheel at the rear. These little carriers weighed about three tons and could be enlarged into light tanks with little extra effort, though they suffered from track problems for years after their inception.

The sale of the Carden-Loyds and their subsequent effect on tank design was quite extraordinary. They were sold all over the world. Russia took several and developed the T-27 and others from them. Italy built the CV–33 and then tried to expand the principle into a medium tank and a self-propelled gun, whereupon it failed. Poland took several and produced the TK–3. Czechoslovakia followed the idea for their MU–124 and France built the UE carriers, all with the Carden-Loyd basis. By the mid-1930s there were many countries who owed the genesis of their armoured force to the purchase of a batch of Carden-Loyd carriers, and even Germany took the general idea when designing the PzKpfw I.

Among the more spectacular products of the inter-war period were the Christie tank designs. J. Walter Christie was an American engineer who had gone into the automobile business in its early days and

Far left, top **The Czech MU-4 machine-gun carrier.** ***Far left, bottom*** **The Polish TK-3 tankette. Both of these were derived from Carden-Loyd designs.** ***Left*** **A Vickers Medium tank and (foreground) a Carden-Loyd carrier in Bovington museum.** ***Upper right*** **A Russian T-27 tankette.** ***Lower right*** **A French Renault UE carrier and trailer.**

who, during World War I, was operating the Front Drive Motor Company. Drawn by the possibility of mounting guns on vehicles, he designed a number of self-propelled mountings which were greeted with some approval by the US Army; but in spite of them encouraging him to continue in this line, in 1918 he dropped artillery and decided to design a tank. This, had the Army but known it, was to be symptomatic of their relationship with Christie until he died in 1944; no sooner had they accepted an idea than Christie was off after some other notion, leaving them the task of perfecting the abandoned design.

Christie's 1919 tank used a very simple design of suspension and incorporated Christie's prime novelty – the track could be removed, whereupon the vehicle could be driven on roads on its wheels. This gave it greater speed and manoeuvrability, and it also saved wear and tear on the tracks, a particularly vulnerable feature of tank design at that time and, to some degree, ever since. The US Army bought this machine and made some tests with it, after which they sent it back to Christie and asked him to make a few changes to bring it closer to the Army's conception of what a tank ought to be. This Christie did, somewhat grudgingly, but further tests with the army showed that it spent more time being repaired than it did being run, and the Army lost interest in it. Christie went ahead on his own, and designed an amphibious tank, one or two of which were bought by the US Marine Corps, and then applied himself to developing a suspension system which would permit high speeds to be attained across country.

In 1928 he offered the US Army a new design in which the tank was carried on a set of large rubber-tyred roadwheels, which touched the track at top and bottom. These were slung on pivoting arms and sprung by large coil springs mounted vertically in the double-skinned hull side, a system which allowed enormous deflection to accommodate rough terrain. As before, it could run with or without its track, and it was propelled by an enormous V–12 aero-engine giving 338hp, which gave the tank the phenomenal speed of 113km/hr (70mph) on wheels (better than many automobiles could manage) or 64km/hr (40mph) on its tracks. Viewed as a tank it was something of an anti-climax, since it was unarmed, though provided with a dummy gun, and the armour was nowhere more than 12mm (½in) thick. But as a spectacular cross-country machine, it enchanted everyone who saw it; the US Army bought five, the Russians bought two, and the Polish Army ordered another two. Christie formed a

Top **An Italian Fiat M28 demonstrating its agility.** ***Centre*** **The Fiat 2000 was the first Italian attempt at a heavy tank.** ***Bottom*** **The German Panzer Kampfwagen I which saw its first combat in Spain.**

new company, the US Wheel and Track-layer Corporation, and all appeared to be going well. The Poles cancelled their order and the US Army bought them instead, but shortly after this the US Ordnance Department fell out again with Christie over contractual terms, and thereafter Christie was by-passed, another company being given orders to build tanks based on the Christie design. A contributory factor is said to have been the fact that the Ordnance Department were less than enchanted at having paid Christie some $800,000 over the previous 12 years without ever receiving a tank which worked properly.

But for all his prickliness and eccentricity, Walter Christie will always be remembered for the suspension system he designed. It was first taken up in quantity by the Soviets, who based their BT series of tanks on it, and later by the British, who based their Cruiser tanks on it. Today it can be found, in modified form, on tanks of every nation.

The Americans were, however, reluctant to embrace the Christie suspension because it was expensive, and in the early 1930s money was everything. Instead, the Rock Island Arsenal persevered in a design of a cheaper form of suspension, known as the volute-spring type. A volute spring can best be described as a ribbon of steel coiled up, and then the inner end thrust out so as to form a tapering coil spring. It acts like a coil spring, but the thickness of the ribbon gives it the degree of stiffness necessary to support the weight of an armoured vehicle. Rock Island perfected this system to such good effect that when World War II came along

and money flowed more or less freely, they elected to stay with it rather than go back to the Christie system; for the tanks of the time it was perfectly adequate, and it was not until after 1943, when performance had increased considerably, that they felt it was worth contemplating the Christie system again.

Less spectacular, but equally vital, was the steady development in most countries of four-wheel-drive vehicles for military use. During World War I a number of four-wheel-drive vehicles were in use. The idea of all-wheel drive had been put forward early in the century as a method of obtaining adequate traction, though not necessarily for cross-country work; there were plenty of roads in those days which were of such poor quality that all-wheel drive was advantageous. Such vehicles as the American FWD, Jeffery, Duplex and Avery were in commercial use prior to 1914 and hundreds were sold to Britain and France once the war began. There they demonstrated their ability to operate off roads, and when the war was over the armies were reluctant to lose this ability. Unfortunately, the 1920s saw improvements in roads to the extent that the all-wheel-drive truck as a commercial proposition almost died out, and so military designers had to work on their own designs. Another factor leading to military design was that commercial all-wheel-drive vehicles, while capable of off-road working, were not really intended for the rough going which military vehicles were called upon to face, and thus the suspension systems were unable to cope with the extreme deflections demanded; only purpose-built military designs offered all the performance which military men wanted.

By the end of the 1920s the design and manufacture of military vehicles had spread around the world, away from its 'traditional' homes, and nowhere was this more notable than in Soviet Russia. Motor vehicles, and particularly the tank, had caught the Soviet imagination – they were forward-looking and technological, and the Soviets were sure that together with aviation and poison gas they were the key to future warfare. Moreover these three fields of development were new ones and there was little 'traditional' background upon which to draw; therefore the Soviets, with application, could be on an equal footing with older nations, everyone being at more or less the same level of competence – and those who worked hardest would come off best.

There was some degree of truth in this theory, but immediately after the Revolution the Soviet nation was in no condition to contemplate research into military science, and it was not until 1928, when the First Five-Year Plan was announced, that any serious work could begin. The First Plan centred on heavy industry and armament production facilities, and part of the target was that, by 1934, the Red Army would have three mechanized brigades, 30 mixed tank battalions, four reserve heavy tank battalions, 13 mechanized

cavalry regiments, and an armoured car company in each infantry division, a grand total of something like 3,500 combat vehicles, plus, of course, the necessary 'soft' vehicles to back all this up. In fact the plan worked so well that by 1933 the Red Army had almost 7,000 tanks alone.

The next stage was the Second Five-Year Plan, which was aimed at completing the entire mechanization of the army. By the end of this plan period (1938) there were over 30 factories producing tanks, armoured cars, trucks and self-propelled guns. One of the lesser problems arising from this vast expansion was the somewhat basic one of providing drivers for all these vehicles; trained drivers were scarce among the annual intake of conscripts and a massive instructional programme had to be launched by para-military training organizations.

CREATIONS OF CHRISTIE

Top left The Medium T4 Convertible tank. *Top right* Walter Christie (standing) with his M1932 tank. *Below* The Christie T3 demonstrates its facility for travelling on either wheels or tracks. Such adaptability was not destined to become the rule.

A notable feature of Soviet vehicle development was that very few specialist military trucks appeared. The standard truck was the GAZ–AA, which was, in fact, the Ford Model AA 1½-ton commercial truck. The Soviets acquired machinery from the German Ford plant in Cologne in the early 1930s and with Ford assistance the GAZ factory at Gorki was built in 1932. The resulting truck was produced by the tens of thousands and applied to almost every military use, even though it lacked four-wheel drive or any other visible military embellishment. Some were converted to half-track form, and a small number of more specialized vehicles, with all-wheel drive, were developed in smaller factories, but the GAZ–AA was to remain a familiar sight in Russian military formations until after World War II.

One field in which the Soviets did excel was in the provision of fully-tracked tractors for artillery. In view of the terrain problems and the Russian climate, this made a great deal of sense, and factories that produced tracked tractors for agricultural purposes found it easy to make slight modifications and produce similar vehicles for the Army. As well as having the virtue of efficiency, another advantage of these tractors was that since they were basically agricultural vehicles, the annual intake of conscripts produced a reasonable number of men who were familiar with them on the farm and who could be converted into artillery drivers with little additional training. Tractors such as the Stalin and Komsomol were little more than truck bodies carried on full-track suspensions, while others such as the Stalinets were purely haulers, closely resembling heavy farm tractors. A further interesting development of these tracked designs was the adaptation of the suspension unit to towed artillery weapons in place of the normal wheels; a free-rolling track unit gave excellent flotation in mud and snow conditions and matched the ability of the tracked tractor to cross difficult country.

The other nation making great advances in the 1930s was, of course, Germany; but although it is generally believed that the German Army was in the forefront of mechanization, as shown by the renowned Panzer divisions, the fact is that they were a good deal less advanced in

Left **The Russian tractor factory at Chelyabinsk: it was a simple matter to convert such plant to tank production.** ***Below right*** **An Italian CV33 tank at Bovington.** ***Bottom*** **The archetypal German half-track, the 'Mittlerer Zugkraftwagen 8-tonne' of 1935.**

basic mechanization of the Army than most other countries. So far behind were they, in fact, that the majority of their field artillery went to war in 1939 behind horse teams.

Where the Germans erred was in trying to over-organize. Where other nations were content to specify a general type of vehicle and let manufacturers come up with their own interpretation, the German Army began by specifying standard chassis for cars and trucks. These were luxurious specifications, to say the least; the car chassis, in three sizes, featured such advanced (and expensive) features as permanent four-wheel drive with limited-slip differentials, independent suspension on all wheels, auxiliary low gears for cross-country work, and two spare wheels mounted on stub axles amidships, where they acted to prevent the car 'bellying' on rough ground. Needless to say, this ideal specification, while producing a splendid vehicle, was not conducive to quantity production, and as a result civilian vehicles of all types were gradually brought into service. This caused complications because of the variety of designs being bought, and before the war a rationalization programme, under Colonel von Schell, was instituted. Each manufacturer was limited to a single basic vehicle of his own design, produced in both two-wheel- and four-wheel-drive models. This brought some sense into military procurement, but even so it would have been better to have had the manufacturers concentrate on one or two vehicles in each class irrespective of who designed them. This, in fact, did take place during the war,

when the standard Opel truck was produced by several factories.

One of the hallmarks of the German Army was the heavy half-tracked towing vehicle used by artillery, and these were developed in a range of sizes and in large numbers. Work on half-tracks began in the 1920s under the hands of several private companies, and in 1926 an extensive trial was carried out to determine the design of artillery tractors. The Army then called for designs of light, medium and heavy tractors and development of these was done by Bussing-NAG, JA Maffei AG and Daimler-Benz, acting under

Tanks preserved in the museum at Bovington: *Below* The German PzKpfw II and *bottom* the French SOMUA S-35. *Opposite* The Matilda I British infantry tank of 1938, well protected but poorly armed.

military guidance. Prototypes were ready by 1932. In 1934 development of lighter types was begun by Borgward and Demag. Eventually design settled down to a pattern using torsion-bar suspension of overlapping wheels in the track unit and models of from one- to eight-ton capacity were produced.

The German Army, like the Soviet, started the inter-war period with the advantage of having no tanks at all; the provisions of the Versailles Treaty denuded them of what few tanks they had owned, and prevented any overt development of fighting vehicles. But behind the scenes a great deal of basic research went on, and in the late 1920s a clandestine testing facility and tank school was operated in Russia with the connivance of the Soviet Army. Experimental chassis were sent to this testing ground and tank commanders and crews were trained in basic tactics and mechanical skills. The principal manufacturers in Germany were given contracts to develop tank chassis under the guise of 'agricultural tractors', and the outcome of these was, firstly, a medium tank known as the 'Neubaufahrzeug' or New Model Vehicle, a 23-tonner with multiple turrets. But since this line of development appeared to proceed too slowly, and since some tanks – any tanks– were needed for training, a design of light tank was pushed forward in 1933. This became the Panzerkampfwagen I and was primarily intended as a cheap training device, though many of them survived to go to war in 1939. This was followed by the PzKpfw II, III and IV models, which formed the basis of the German Panzer divisions by the outbreak of war in 1939.

British development during the between-wars years was hampered by lack of finance and much of the early tank work was done by Vickers, working to specifications laid down by the War Office. This led to light and medium types being taken into service, though never in adequate numbers, and it also led to Vickers building up a sizeable export trade in designs not far removed from those issued to British service. Many of these Vickers models served to start other countries on their tank-development programmes; Russia and Japan both purchased Vickers tanks in the 1920s and, after testing and studying them, went on to develop their own ideas, having saved a great deal of time and money by escaping the initial stages of design.

Britain also made some notable steps in the development of supporting specialist vehicles, though again the shortage of money prevented many of these being adopted in large numbers. A self-propelled gun, known as the Birch Gun, appeared in 1927, using an 18-pounder field piece mounted in a revolving turret. It was then redesigned to carry the gun in an open barbette, which allowed it to function as an anti-aircraft gun with some success. But due to disputes over the tactical handling of armour, as well as the lack of cash, this line of development petered out and the guns were scrapped in the early 1930s.

The Royal Artillery appear to have been rather less resistant to the idea of mechanization than most other horsed units, and several artillery tractors were produced. Notable among these was the Hathi (Hindustani for elephant), which was first made by a military unit by cannibalizing parts of some captured German four-wheel-drive tractors. It proved to be successful, and commercial models were later made by Thorneycroft in 4 × 4 and 6 × 6 versions. This line of development eventually led to the 4 × 4 Guy Quad Ant, which was to become the standard field artillery tractor throughout World War II. It might be said here that there was a certain amount of opposition to the idea of developing a specialized gun tractor for field artillery use; the line of counter-argument was that such vehicles were useless for anything else, being unsuited to load-carrying since they consisted entirely of crew space and ammunition lockers. Their opponents would have preferred the artillery to use standard cargo trucks as

towing vehicles, so that once the guns were emplaced the trucks could be used for other tasks. But the artillery, in their wisdom, knew that once trucks are removed for other tasks they prove exceedingly difficult to recall when the guns require shifting, and they managed to retain their 'quads' until well after World War II.

In spite of America's wide-scale adoption of the automobile, the US Army moved slowly on the road to mechanization. This was due to the same two brakes which were to be found in other countries – lack of money and a powerful cavalry clique in the higher echelons of military decision-making. Another drawback was peculiarly American, in that when the United States Army was reconstituted by the 1920 National Defence Act, the wartime Tank Corps was disbanded and tanks were allocated to infantry; as a result, tank design tended to be tied to what the infantry thought a tank should do, which was largely walk alongside the infantryman and protect him. On the other hand, when some of the more forward-looking elements of the cavalry wanted to experiment with armoured vehicles, they were hamstrung by the 'tanks = infantry' edict, an impasse which was eventually resolved by the fiction of calling all cavalry vehicles 'combat cars', irrespective of whether they ran on wheels or tracks. In many cases the infantry's tank and the cavalry's combat car were identical.

A little-known facet of American military vehicle development was that represented by a quasi-official body known as the Army Ordnance Association. This had been formed after 1918 as 'an organization of American citizens pledged to industrial preparedness for war' and which endeavoured 'to keep alive an interest in and knowledge of the design, production and maintenance of munitions...' Many of its members were in responsible industrial posts, and there was thus an interchange of information between the military and industry. The association also brought the Society of Automotive Engineers into contact with the Ordnance Department, another extremely valuable piece of cross-fertilization. As a result of these contacts and interchanges, industry was constantly aware of what the Army needed, while the Army were kept informed of fresh industrial developments. True, the Army still had little money with which to pursue its chosen paths, but in many cases manufacturers were able to overlook this and, with their own development funds, help the army to at least a pilot model or prototype. In this way such things as heavy multi-wheel-drive trucks, armoured cars, half-track vehicles and artillery tractors of various patterns were tested; while few were ever carried beyond a single model, they nevertheless gave the Army valuable data

With few exceptions, American tank (and combat car) design was in the hands of the US Ordnance Department, and most of the work was carried out at their Rock Island Arsenal. Few American manufacturers seemed interested in developing tanks – probably because they felt there was little market demand for them – and, in any case, the Ordnance Department were a trifle wary of outside designers after the experiences with Walter Christie. Apart from Christie himself, only the Marmon-Herrington company engaged in tank design and they were largely concerned with producing light armoured vehicles for sale to South American countries; in addition to this, though, they were able to build occasional vehicles to Ordnance specification, as did Cunningham from time to time.

Below **The Soviet SU-100 self-propelled gun, an excellent assault gun and tank destroyer in 1944/5.** ***Facing page*** **A Crossley-Chevrolet armoured car of the type used in the Western Desert campaign 1940/1.**

The Second World War

AFTER THE OUTBREAK OF WAR in 1939, and with the spectre of the (apparently) highly mechanized German Panzer divisions in front of them, the various nations of the world, who were either engaged in the war or looking on, all began to overhaul their mechanization programmes with the utmost rapidity. Tanks and armoured cars had to be produced, and with them the trucks and tractors to keep the rest of the army on the move in what promised to be a mobile war. The totalitarian nations began in a strong position, having been able to build up their tank forces and ancillaries before the war, while the democracies were in their usual starting condition, starved of equipment. In the long run, the advantages reversed themselves, in that the countries with vast stocks of tanks tended to hang on to what they had and continue to use them long after they should have been replaced, confident in the belief that the superiority they enjoyed at the commencement of the war would see them through to the end. On the other hand, the countries with little equipment at the start were able to hang on with what they had while designers and manufacturers got to work on fresh models, so that towards the mid-point of the war there was a qualitative overhauling of the other side. This, in its turn, led to another burst of activity, and design, especially of tanks, turned into a leapfrog progression, first one side and then the other gaining the upper hand.

The reason for all this was, of course, that tank design had proceeded more or less in a vacuum for 20 years; very few people had any firm ideas on how tanks ought to be handled in war and, therefore, how tank design should be specified, and the few who did have ideas were generally out of agreement between themselves. The 'small wars' such as the Spanish Civil War, the Italian invasion of Abyssinia and the Japanese activities in Manchuria and China had been productive of some very conflicting lessons and really left no one the wiser. It was not until after the Polish campaign of 1939 that reliable conclusions could be drawn, conclusions which were largely reinforced by the events in France during the summer of 1940.

The first thing to become apparent was that the light tank, beloved in pre-war

days for its cheapness, was of no use at all on a modern battlefield, since it could not survive against either larger tanks or anti-tank weapons. The British, quick off the mark for once, abandoned them forthwith (except as driver-training vehicles), but the Americans and Germans kept them in service for some time; the former because light tanks were all they had at the manufacturing stage, and the latter because abandoning light tanks would have halved their armoured strength at one stroke. Both, therefore, had to hold on to their tanks until they could find something heavier with which to replace them, and in the end the Americans, because their light tanks were heavier and stronger than anyone else's, kept theirs in use until 1945.

The second thing to become apparent was that the whole design ethos of the tank required examination; the tank was a combination of three things, mobility, firepower and protection, and in pre-war days most designers had put mobility first, protection second and firepower last. Events in France showed that henceforth the three qualities had to be at least evenly divided or had to have more accent on protection and firepower, since mobility alone was not enough, as the demise of the light tank proved. The epitome of this was the brief action at Arras in 1940, when the Germans came up against the British

Matilda II tank; this was, for its day, exceedingly heavily armoured, and the normal German anti-tank and tank weapons made no impression on it. Only the last-minute deployment of a troop of 88mm anti-aircraft guns as anti-tank weapons saved the day for the Germans. From this, and from later experiments upon captured Matildas, they deduced that more armour and better guns were the priorities. The British, however, over-looked the conclusions to be drawn from Arras for some time, and continued to stress mobility, so that when armoured warfare was resumed in the western desert in 1941-2 the German tanks outgunned the British by a considerable margin. The other defect in British tanks at this time was a certain lack of mechanical reliability, due to the lack of a coherent design policy in pre-war days; instead of concentrating on a basic design and bringing it to

Facing page top **A Soviet T-26 light tank is blessed before going into action in Spain, 1938.** ***Facing page centre*** **A British Matilda MkIII infantry tank.** ***Facing page bottom*** **A Matilda MkII at Bovington Museum.** ***Below*** **A Soviet T-34 Medium tank with 76mm gun and, behind, an SU-100 assault gun.**

perfection, the British, blown hither and yon by constantly changing tactical policies, had abandoned a line of research to chase after another, without perfecting any of them.

The only people who had been able to afford the luxury of chasing innumerable designs had been the Soviets, who, with their massive mechanization programme, had the money and facilities to pursue several avenues of approach. As a result, by 1939 they had a wide variety of tanks in service, most of which were obsolescent, but at least they had a firm idea of what was required. A high-powered diesel engine had been developed and perfected over five years by the Kharkov Locomotive Works; a high-velocity 76mm gun was also perfected; and experience in Spain and Manchuria (in border incidents with the Japanese) had shown that riveted armour was dangerous to the occupants of the tank and that welded armour had now to be used. Furthermore the armour had to be sloped so as to deflect projectiles instead of presenting a face at right-angles to the shot's trajectory. With all these things in mind the Soviet designers sat down and produced the T–34 medium tank, one of the outstanding designs of history. Production began in May 1940 and because the design was sound from the outset it continued in production throughout the war, a total of 39,698 being built. In similar vein a heavy tank was designed and put into production as the 'Klim Voroshilov'; this was less successful than the T–34, but several thousand were built and it formed the starting point for development, which led to more formidable heavy tanks later in the war.

When the Germans attacked Russia in June 1941 it is doubtful whether the Soviets had as many as a thousand of their two new designs in service, and these were scattered across Russia in 'penny packets'. As a result, the German advance was countered by older designs, and the Panzers shot these out of the way without very much trouble. But within two weeks of the start of the campaign there were reports which presaged trouble; the first came from a unit of Von Manstein's 56th Corps, who reported that an enormous and apparently shot-proof Russian tank of unknown design had suddenly appeared astride a supply route and had, for several hours, stood off every German attempt to dislodge it. Attempts to bring an 88mm

gun into action had been beaten off by the tank's powerful gun, and eventually a major diversion had to be staged to draw the tank into an ambush, where the '88' could destroy it. This was the German's introduction to the KV tank. Shortly after this the 17th Panzer Division reported a 'strange and low-slung tank of formidable appearance' which had emerged from some woods close to the Dniepr river and, with German shot bouncing from its armour, had ploughed a nine-mile swathe of destruction through the German lines until it was stopped by a medium artillery gun which it had inadvertently missed. That was the first appearance of the T–34.

Once the invasion had begun, the

Facing page, left **A Soviet KVII heavy tank.** ***Facing page bottom*** **A Sherman flail tank clearing mines in Normandy, 1944.** ***Across centre*** **The American 'Aunt Jemima' mine-clearing roller, in use with the 6th US Army in 1945.** ***Below*** **A Sherman Crab, stowing the flail apparatus.** ***Lower left*** **Front view of a Matilda Scorpion in action.** ***Lower right*** **A Sherman Crab at work.**

Soviets, with admirable single-mindedness, abandoned plans for all other tanks except the KV and T–34 and set about building them as hard as they could. This plan was all but ruined by the fact that the German advance had overrun the tank arsenals in Kharkov, Zhdanov and Kirov; but as the German advance neared these plants every scrap of machinery which could be got out was loaded on to railway trains and rushed east to Chelyabinsk. Here the evacuated factories were amalgamated to form a huge combine called 'Tankograd', and within two months new KVs were in production. Another group of evacuated factories became the 'Uralmashzavod' (Ural machinery factory) at Nizhni Tagil, and set about turning out T–34s. By 1943 there were 43 factories across Russia doing nothing but turn out KV and T–34 tanks, and it has been said, with some truth, that by 1944 the Russians could make tanks faster than the Germans could destroy them.

In similar fashion, enormous factories were set up to produce trucks. The ZIS factory in Moscow was relocated in the Urals and went on turning out standard three-ton 4 × 2 cargo trucks, $2\frac{1}{2}$-ton 4 × 4 trucks and minor variations on these two basic designs for use as engineer vehicles, searchlight trucks and similar specialist types. The GAZ factory was also relocated and produced cars, trucks and ambulances. But the weight of Soviet effort went on tanks and fighting vehicles, to the extent that over 400,000 trucks were shipped from the USA under the Lend-Lease scheme to keep the Red Army mobile.

That the Americans could afford to supply such a vast number of vehicles is testimony to their mass-production expertise in the automotive field and also testimony to the Ordnance Department's policy of standardizing certain basic types of vehicle early in the war and then simply allowing the manufacturers to turn them out as fast as they could go. As indicated above, much of the pre-war period had been occupied in determining the basic parameters of different types of vehicle, so that by 1939-40 the Ordnance Department were in a position to be able to lay down specifications and know that they would work. As a result, the USA undoubtedly became the 'Arsenal of Democracy' in the motor vehicle field, with over 3,000,000 military transport vehicles, 88,410 tanks, 41,170 half-tracks, 82,000 tractors and several thousand other specialist vehicles.

The two American vehicles that were probably more widely distributed and best known of all were the Jeep and the Deuce-and-a-half or Jimmy. A total of 639,245 Jeeps were built, while almost a million Jimmy trucks were made, and there are quite a few of both types still in use around the world. The Jeep – more properly the 'Truck, ¼-ton, 4 × 4 Command & Reconnaissance' – arose from an Ordnance demand in 1940 for a light car to pull the 37mm anti-tank gun and carry its crew. The first vehicle to appear was designed by the American Bantam Company, and this was followed by designs from the Willys and Ford companies. The specification called for the vehicle to weigh no more than 600kg (1,300lb), but the Willys company ignored this since they considered it to be ill-founded, leading to an underpowered and understrength result. They were quite right, and the revised specification increased the weight limit to 975kg (2,150lb). The Willys design, having the most powerful engine, was accepted, becoming the Model MA, while the same vehicle, built by Ford, became the Model GPW, from which arose the name Jeep.

The Deuce-and-a-half was the 2½-ton 6 × 6 cargo truck produced by the General Motors Corporation (GMC – hence Jimmy) from 1941 onwards. The size was considered to be the heaviest truck which could be mass-produced, and the demand was so great that Studebaker and International Harvester were also engaged in manufacturing to the same design. As well as the basic cargo model, there were innumerable variations based on the same chassis.

When tank production was first mooted in 1939 the Ordnance Department turned to the heavy engineering industry, considering that they would have the required expertise in handling heavy casting and large assemblies. As a result the first tank contracts went to firms such as the American Locomotive Company, the Lima Locomotive Company and the Baldwin Locomotive Company, and it is to their credit that they met their targets and produced the tanks on time. But in June 1940, William S. Knudsen, President of General Motors, suggested that the automobile industry had more experience at mass-production and ought to be called in. Since by this time the locomotive companies were working at full stretch and there was still an expansion in tank

Facing page **A Jeep ferries a surrender party up to the leading tank of the US 4th Armored Division in Germany, 1945.** ***Below left*** **An American Light tank M2 in 1939.** ***Below right*** **A Marmon-Herrington Light tank used by the US Army in the Aleutian Islands, 1942.** ***Bottom*** **An M3 General Grant Medium tank at Bovington Museum.**

production envisaged, the Army agreed and Knudsen contacted K. T. Keller, President of the Chrysler Corporation, to ask if Chrysler would take on the task of setting up a complete tank factory and running it for the Government. After examining the drawings of the proposed tank, Chrysler produced their plans for a 21 million dollar arsenal in Detroit; building began in September, and in April 1941 the arsenal turned out its first tank.

The tank they turned out, however, was not the tank they had contracted to make; a great deal had happened in those seven months.

At the start of 1940 the Americans had a light tank entering production and a medium tank on the drawing board; the latter, the M2A1, was completed in May, almost on the day that the German advance through France and Belgium began. In June the National Munitions Program was introduced, which called for, among other things, 1,741 medium tanks to be produced in the next 18 months. It was this which led to the idea of the Detroit Arsenal, and the drawings upon which the Chrysler engineers based their plans were those of the M2A1 medium tank. But while the Chrysler men were poring over these, the Army, after studying reports of the fighting in Europe, came to the conclusion that the 37mm gun of the M2A1 was insufficient and that the medium tank had to have a 75mm gun. While the Ordnance Department agreed in principle, they had to point out that the turret of the M2A1 was too small for a 75mm gun; an entirely new turret would be required, of a size never before attempted in America, and, of course, the hull would have to be altered to suit. While they were happy to go ahead and design a suitable tank, this would take time, and meanwhile here were Chrysler with 21 million dollars and a contract for a thousand tanks. The solution to this impasse was to make a minimal redesign of the M2A1: to put a 75mm gun into a sponson on one side of the hull, shift the turret over slightly, and retain the 37mm gun in the turret. This would require the minimum amount of redesign and would provide the army with an interim tank. The idea was accepted and became the M3 medium tank; the contract with Chrysler was torn up in favour of an identical contract for 1,000 M3s. Chrysler now had the immense problem of having to design their factory piecemeal as they received drawings of the latest modifications, and the final drawings were not received until March 1941, three weeks before the first pilot model of the M3 was completed.

The new design with the 75mm gun in the turret turned out to be the famous M4 medium, more commonly known as the Sherman tank, the tank which became, in effect, the Allied standard tank for the rest of the war, since it became the backbone of both American and British armoured units. The Americans were fond of saying that they would 'Win the War with the Sherman', the aim being to fasten on a sound design, modify it as little as possible and turn it out in overwhelming numbers, very much as the Soviets did with their T-34. Unfortunately, the Sherman wasn't a T-34. Had the war ended a year sooner, the Sherman would have lived up to its promoters' hopes, but by the time the Sherman came into full combat use, in 1944–5, the design was four years old and the 75mm gun, which had looked so formidable in 1940, was outclassed by German guns and outmatched by German armour.

To the credit of the Ordnance Department, they had foreseen this and as early as 1940 they had begun work on a heavy tank armed with a 3in gun. This became the M6, an excellent vehicle in many respects and one which would have served well in Europe given a few up-dating modifications. But for reasons never satisfactorily explained the higher echelons of the US Army turned it down and effectively stifled the production of any sort of heavy tank until late in 1944, when it was belatedly realized that a heavy tank was desperately needed in Europe. Since the Ordnance Department had quietly continued to develop a heavy design throughout the war, they were able to produce a suitable tank design off the shelf, but it took time to get into production and the US heavy tank did not appear on the battlefield until the last few weeks of the war and then in insufficient numbers.

One factor contributing to the peculiarly short-sighted attitude over heavy tanks was the American dictum that tanks as such were 'exploitation' vehicles, intended to carry the advance through the enemy defensive line; their job was not, however, to fight other tanks; that was supposed to be left to tank destroyers, specialized armour which fell into the self-propelled gun class. Many and varied, weird and wonderful were the tank destroyers which proliferated in 1940–2 in America; everything from redundant anti-aircraft guns on crawler tractors (with no room for gun crew or ammunition) via obsolete 'French 75' field-pieces on minimal wheeled chassis to 105mm howitzers inserted into armoured cars. Eventually some sanity prevailed and the standardized tank destroyer became the M10, a 3in anti-tank gun in an open-topped turret on a Sherman chassis. This had to be given a more powerful gun before it was really effective, and with that it performed as well as could be asked; but there was always a tendency for the crews to try and use the vehicle as a tank, while there were never enough tank destroyers to take the burden of tank fighting away from the plain tanks entirely. It was not until the war was over that the Americans finally recognized that tanks had to be able to deal with anything which crossed their path and that the artificial demarcation between tanks and tank destroyers had to go.

In September 1939 the British Army mustered some 85,000 motor vehicles, but of that total no fewer than 21,500 were motorcycles and over 26,000 of the vehicles were impressed civilian cars, trucks and motorcycles. Much of this

Below **Maintenance time on an M4 Sherman. This vehicle's suspension and tracks in particular required frequent adjustment.**

strength was left behind in France in 1940, and as a result the British motor industry worked overtime to make up the deficit and provide the wheels which the army needed. In general, the designs produced were all pre-war in origin and they served well enough. Specialized vehicles were developed on the standard types of chassis, notably in the ¾-ton and three-ton ranges, while most of the heavier cargo trucks were no more than lightly disguised civilian patterns. It was not until 1943, when production had more or less caught up with demand, that manufacturers and military design establishments began to produce new ideas, though all too often some of these were merely copies of foreign design; there were, for example, several attempts to produce a vehicle comparable to the Jeep, there were copies of the American Dodge ¾-ton weapons carrier, and copies of the German Krauss-Maffei ¾-tracked gun tractor. On the other hand some of the projects were eminently practical, or would have been had they started in 1938 instead of 1943, so that they could have been brought to fruition in time to be of some use. One such idea was the Octolat, an eight-wheeled cargo carrier-cum-artillery tractor capable of crossing the most formidable terrain; the war ended before this idea could be perfected, but it is probable that it formed the inspiration for, and some of the background to, the later Stalwart multi-wheel cargo carrier.

In the design and development of tanks, Britain's record makes pitiful reading; the 1946 Report of the Select Committee for National Expenditure was forthright enough to say that 'no tank produced in 1943 was worthy of action, while those manufactured earlier were inferior, both technically and tactically, to German tanks'. The reasons for this are involved and cannot be fully explored here, for it would take up too much space. In broad terms, it can be said that the failure to produce a decent tank stemmed from a combination of lack of guidance from the General Staff and the various branches of the Army as to precisely what was required; the lack of a powerful production engine and the reluctance of the British motor industry to develop one; and political interference, which led to the breaking up of the system of design and development shortly before the war in order to construct a new Minstry of Supply. As a result of this latter move, tank design went into the hands of a largely civilian committee, which regarded the tank as being primarily an automotive device and which gave little consideration to its fighting aspects, resulting in designs which were undergunned for most of the war. The sudden rush into rearmament in the late 1930s, coupled with the simultaneous reorganization of the whole procedure for design and production, led to a number of hastily conceived designs which, in service, proved to be mechanically unreliable. Of one design it has to be written: 'After 70 miles the gearbox gave out and by the end of December [six weeks later] forty-seven mechanical failures had been reported, while the steering brakes had a life of only 127 miles. By April...their performance was being reckoned in miles per transmission...' Yet because nothing better was available, this design had to be made to work, became the Crusader tank, and over 6,000 were built. Five years later, in the desert war, it was still unreliable.

In desperation (or so it seems in retrospect) the Tank Board welcomed any design which appeared to promise success; the Covenanter appeared, designed by a railway engineer, and proved no more reliable than the Crusader, while its crews detested it because the designer, for reasons which he doubtless felt were good, put the radiator inside the fighting compartment 'where it accomplished the dual role of cooling the engine and roasting the crew'. Even worse was the TOG, designed by a team of men who had been responsible for the tanks of World War I and who, it seemed, had learned nothing since.

Part of the trouble seems to have arisen due to the artificial demarcation of British tanks into light, cruiser and Infantry types; the light were supposed to reconnoitre, the cruiser to swoop about the battlefield to disrupt enemy communications, raid headquarters and perform such deeds as had been the prerogative of cavalry raids in days gone by, while the infantry tank was heavily armoured and ponderous to suit its role of accompanying the infantryman at walking pace across No Man's Land. This theory led designers into some fearful blind alleys, but worst of all was its

Facing page, top **A British Crusader tank, mainstay of the British Army until the arival of the General Lee.** ***Facing page, bottom*** **The 17-pounder Archer self-propelled gun, with a General Patton in the background.** ***Below left*** **A Churchill MkVI preserved at Bovington.** ***Below right*** **The TOG Mark 24 with 17-pounder gun.** ***Bottom*** **A Cromwell IV of 1944.**

effect on gun policy; the logic ran thus: a light tank is to reconnoitre, therefore it does not need a powerful gun; the cruiser is for raiding, therefore it does not need a powerful gun; the infantry tank will be impervious, therefore it does not need a powerful gun. Although the gun designers saw the fallacies of this, they were unable to persuade the tank designers to make turrets large enough to take powerful weapons, with the result that British tanks were armed with the two-pounder (40mm) gun long after the Germans had gone to 50mm and even 75mm and the Americans had settled on 75mm as being the minimum feasible size.

In tank design generally, the turning point came when the Germans began to be confronted with growing numbers of Soviet T–34 and KV tanks. These were all but impervious to most German weapons except at suicidally short ranges, and it became imperative for the Germans to overhaul both their tanks and their anti-tank armament. Strangely, tank design in Germany had virtually stood still since 1939, largely because of a misguided belief that the war would be over so quickly that there would not be time to develop and produce fresh designs. Consequently, when in 1942 the German Army began making agitated noises, it took time to get the machinery of design and development turning over. Indeed, the first response was the suggestion that the Germans should simply make a carbon copy of the T–34, but this, being impractical for many manufacturing reasons, was turned down. The final result was the design of the Panther and Tiger tanks, two formidable vehicles both in the scale of their protection and in their armament, the former having a high-velocity 75mm gun and the latter a tank version of the celebrated 88mm anti-aircraft gun. But in spite of the best efforts of the designers, the German engineering industry was in no shape to perform prodigies of production, and the total number of Tiger and Panther tanks turned out before the war ended was less than 7,000.

By making the qualitative leap-frog, however, the Panther and Tiger designs spurred the various Allies to overhaul

their own designs and, in their turn, make the next leap-frog move. The Soviets, relying greatly on the speed and agility of the T–34 and overwhelming production, left the tank more or less as it was, but concentrated on improving the armament, going up to an 85mm gun. In the KV series they were less happy, since it had not proved quite as good as they had hoped, and a complete redesign was done to produce the Josef Stalin, with ample protection and a devastating 122mm gun. The British, in a masterpiece of improvisation, managed to shoe-horn their 17-pounder gun into a Sherman turret to develop the Firefly tank and began design of the Comet, which was to carry a derated 17-pounder. The Americans, finally convinced that the 75mm gun was no longer master of all it met, tried a number of expedients before settling on a 76mm gun as their main tank armament. This gave about 50 percent better performance than the 75mm, but was still not enough to cope with Panther or Tiger at fighting ranges and, to boot, kicked up such a fearful blast and cloud of dust as to preclude the chance of a quick second shot. The British suggested adopting their idea of mounting the 17-pounder gun, while the Armored Force asked for a 90mm gun derived from an anti-aircraft gun, but neither suggestion appeared acceptable to the Ordnance Department and it took a great deal of

Far left **An action sequence showing the tank/infantry team in action in Russia, 1942.** ***Centre*** **A PzKpfw IV with short 75mm gun.** ***Below*** **A PzKpfw IV in Russia, 1942.** ***Lower left*** **A King Tiger with Porsche turret.** ***Lower right*** **A Tiger I of 1942. Both these tigers are caged at Bovington.**

struggle to get them to change their ideas; finally they adopted the 90mm gun in their heavy tank, but they left the Sherman perilously undergunned to the last.

The armoured car, that earliest of armoured vehicles, had a mixed reception during the war years. As a fighting vehicle, it came into the same category as the light tank and suffered from the same basic defect – it could no longer survive in the face of tanks or anti-tank guns. But as a reconnaissance vehicle, seeking information about enemy dispositions and evading combat where possible, it still performed a valuable function, particularly during the desert war of 1941–2. Britain therefore developed some good armoured cars and America began to follow suit. But once the war left the wide open spaces of the desert and moved on to the European mainland, the armoured car proved less serviceable, since it was all too easily ambushed in close or built-up country. From 1943, therefore, the demand for armoured cars was reduced, though they were still used until the war ended. In 1940–1 an immense number of armoured car designs appeared in the USA, largely because they offered a quick and easy solution to the problem of putting a protected gun on wheels, but far too many of them were hopelessly impractical. For example, there was the Baker Jumping Car which had the wheels carried on powerful springs and which, it was claimed, could jump over 1.20m (4ft) obstacles; there was the Trackless Tank, an eight-wheeled monster armed with only a 37mm gun, though it was later improved by putting a 3in gun on to it. In general, there seemed to be confusion in the minds of the designers; they were not quite sure whether they were producing armoured cars or self-propelled guns.

This page, top **Ferdinand or 'Elefant'.** ***This page, lower*** **A captured Sturmgeschutz, France 1944.** ***Facing page, top left*** **An American M7 self-propelled 105mm howitzer.** ***Far right, top*** **Infantry cluster around the turret of a Sherman M4.** ***Far right, lower*** **A Canadian Ram tank, with a 6-pounder gun.** ***Facing page, lower*** **The 'Bishop' 25-pounder self-propelled gun.**

Eventually a special board of review, the Palmer Board, sat during the winter of 1942–3, reviewed all the designs on offer and threw most of them out. One useful decision of this board was that nothing over seven tons in weight could be contemplated as an armoured car.

The major automotive growth area of the war period was the self-propelled gun. This was virtually ignored before the war and the first move was a request from the German Panzer troops, in 1938, for an assault gun, a tracked and armoured vehicle carrying a heavier gun than that commonly found on tanks and capable of accompanying assaulting infantry so as to deal with any strongpoint or obstacles which held them up. What evolved from this was a tank chassis with a superstructure raised slightly above the hull level and roofed over, with a 75mm infantry gun mounted firing forward and with limited traverse. The vehicle had no turret, and this alone made it a cheaper and easier vehicle to produce than the comparable tank. It was followed by several variant designs, adapting miscellaneous chassis to the same task or improving the gun power by the use of bigger calibres – the Germans found that captured tanks were a fruitful source of chassis for these weapons. From this design they moved to developing tank destroyers along similar lines, making them more massively armoured and with more powerful guns, a line of development which culminated in the Ferdinand or Elefant mounting a powerful 88mm gun. This vehicle showed up the basic drawback of tank destroyers of this type; whilst it was a formidable weapon which could demolish anything within the traversing range of its gun, it was virtually defenceless and blind outside that arc, and it proved all too easy for infantry tank-hunters to creep up on the 'blind' side and destroy the Elefant with hand-placed charges.

While the Germans (and Russians, too, who copied the idea) relied upon close-range assault guns, the British and Americans regarded self-propelled artillery from an entirely different point of view. Their main demand was to equip the standard support artillery so that it could keep up with the speed of an armoured advance, deploy rapidly and pull out of position equally rapidly. Towed artillery, particularly in medium calibres (about 155mm), was slow across country and took time to go into and come out of

action. The first serious move in this direction was the British development of Bishop, a Valentine tank chassis upon which was placed a large steel box mounting a 25-pounder field gun. Due to the construction of the armoured box, the gun could only elevate to 15°, which restricted its fighting range to 5,850m (6,400yds) instead of the normal 12,225m (13,400yds) of the field gun. One hundred of these were built in late 1941 and were used in North Africa, but apart from imparting some useful instruction on the tactical handling of self-propelled guns, they were not particularly impressive.

In November 1941 the Americans mounted their 105mm howitzer, their

standard field piece, on to a modified M3 Grant tank chassis; the superstructure was open-topped and built up at the sides into an armoured enclosure, and through the front plate of this the howitzer protruded. Alongside the howitzer was a round pulpit-like structure which mounted an anti-aircraft machine gun, and it was the appearance of this which led the British troops to christen it Priest, conforming to the ecclesiastical tradition begun with Bishop. This, the Howitzer Motor Carriage M7, was used by the British in the desert and in Italy and by the Americans in all theatres and proved to be a most successful vehicle. In British service it was only disliked because it demanded a special supply of ammunition, since 105mm was not a British calibre, and the British asked for a similar conversion but mounting the 25-pounder gun. The Americans produced a prototype which resembled the M7, but somewhat marred the effect by pointing out that, of course, American production facilities could not be utilized to make a machine which the Americans themselves would not use. So the idea was taken across the border to Canada, where a factory had been set up to produce the Ram tank, more or less a Canadian version of the M3; this had turned out less successfully than expected, largely because of the British insistence on undergunning it, and so the facilities were turned over to making a self-propelled gun out of the chassis and mounting the 25-pounder on it. This became Sexton, which served with the British Army until the 1950s and is still serving the Portuguese and other armies.

While putting the divisional field piece on tracks satisfied the British at the time, it didn't satisfy the Americans, and they next turned to the problem of moving their medium artillery. The M12 gun was the result of this, and it broke new ground by simply being a mobile platform for the gun – there was no armour or protection for the crew. This made sense, since no one in his right mind was going to dash into the thick of battle with a 155mm medium gun; it was an indirect-fire weapon pure and simple, and putting it on tracks simply improved its mobility and speed of response by several orders of magnitude. An innovation on this chassis was the use of a bulldozer-like blade at the rear end which, dropped so as to dig into the ground, took the shock of firing from the suspension. The only defect of the whole equipment was that it had been designed around an obsolete weapon, the 155mm M1918 gun, stocks of which were rapidly running out. So a fresh design was begun using the new M1 gun and basing it on the chassis of the M4 Sherman tank; parallel with this was a sister design using the 8in howitzer on the same chassis. Both these entered service shortly before the war ended and continued to serve for many years in both British and American armies.

The American designers, having got the bit firmly between their teeth, then went on to develop self-propelled carriages for the 240mm howitzer and the 8in long-range gun; five of the former and two of

Left **The German SdKfz 2 tracked motorcycle unit used as a light utility vehicle.** ***Below*** **American LVTs leaving a beach.** ***Facing page*** **A British FV432 armoured personnel carrier swimming, demonstrating the Straussler system of obtaining additional buoyancy by means of a canvas screen.**

the latter were built, intended for shipment to the Pacific for use in the forthcoming invasion of Japan, but the end of the war arrived before they had been approved for service and they were all scrapped shortly afterwards

One last category of vehicle which must be mentioned in connection with World War II is that of amphibians. Strategic demands dictated that much of the major action of the war, from the Allies' point of view, had to take place after landing on a hostile beach, and it was too much to expect that it would be possible to land all the many types of vehicles dryshod. Therefore a certain proportion had to be designed to swim ashore so as to provide the landing troops with immediate support and supplies. Moreover, once ashore there would be rivers to cross where no bridges existed. Some desultory work on amphibians had been done before the war, but it was the prospect of making landings on remote islands in the Pacific and on the shores of Europe which concentrated the designers' minds from about 1941 onward.

The US Marines had been investigating the techniques of beach landings throughout the 1920s and 1930s, and in 1924 they had tried two Christie amphibious tanks off Puerto Rico, though without much success. In 1932, however, a retired engineer named Roebling began developing a vehicle intended for rescue work in the Florida Everglades, and he eventually developed an aluminium-bodied tracked vehicle which could cross land on its tracks and also paddle itself through the water. Roebling's Alligator was featured in the press, and in 1940 the Marine Corps ordered three. After tests, they decided that this was the vehicle for which they had been searching and

ordered another 200, calling them their LVT–1 (Landing Vehicle Tracked 1). It was followed by LVT–2, and then by a much improved design, LVT–3, which had a stern ramp through which stores and men, even a Jeep, could be loaded. The next step, dictated by combat conditions, was to add armour and finally to fit some LVTs with tank turrets so that they could act as support weapons. Some 18,000 of the various LVT models were eventually made, and their contribution to the war in the Pacific theatre was immeasurable.

In addition to their use in the Pacific, LVTs were also seen in the European theatre, notably in northern Italy and in the inundated areas of the Low Countries. In these conditions, as in the sheltered lagoons of tropical islands, they were quite adequate, but when it came to crossing the English Channel, the LVT was outclassed and some other ideas had to be canvassed. A certain number of LVTs might be carried by larger ships and launched off shore, but the greatest problem was going to be actually fighting ashore, a task which needed massive firepower and immediate support. Somehow tanks had to be swum ashore, since it was unlikely that the heavy tank landing craft would be able to get close enough to the beach to allow the tanks to simply wade through shallow water.

The prospect of trying to make 20 or 30 tons of tank float was a daunting one, but the answer lay in artificially increasing its displacement to make it buoyant. This was done by Nicholas Straussler, an engineer who had been involved in armoured car design before the war and who now developed the DD (Duplex Drive) tank This was an ordinary tank – a Sherman, for example – with a collapsible canvas screen attached all round the hull. This could be raised by applying compressed air to 36 tubular rubber pillars, and, once raised, it could be secured by steel struts. This gave the tank floating capability, and water propulsion was provided by two propellers, driven through the motion of the tracks and rear idler wheels, which could be lowered into position and then retracted when the tank arrived on shore. Once ashore, the steel struts were unlocked by a hydraulic system and the compressed air was released from the pillars so that the screen collapsed and the tank's gun had a clear field of fire. DD tanks were made in both Britain and the USA and were used with success in the D-Day landings and, after that, in the crossings of the Rhine and Elbe.

Below **The British FV439 armoured personnel carrier mounting a 120mm Wombat anti-tank gun.** ***Facing page, top*** **American T114 armoured personnel carrier with experimental cannon.** ***Facing page, bottom*** **British FV439, a specialised conversion of the standard APC for use as a radio communications centre.**

THE POST-WAR YEARS

AFTER THE WAR ENDED the immediate reaction on the part of Britain and America was to disband their immense forces and return to normal as soon as possible, and in that sort of atmosphere little thought was given to future developments. But within a very short time it became apparent that things were never going to 'get back to normal' and military preparedness was something which was going to have to continue indefinitely. The British had, at last, produced a serviceable tank in the Centurion, just as the war was ending, and this was continually improved and developed in the post war years. The Soviets had produced their Josef Stalin III at the Berlin victory parade, and the heavy sloped armour and massive gun on this tank gave rise to questions of parity and led to work in Britain and the USA on a new generation of tanks with comparable armament.

So far as soft-skinned vehicles went, so many had been produced during the war that most countries were living on their fat for several years, and American surplus

This page, from top **Tracked Rapier AA Missile; US M113 APC.** ***Centre*** **British Chieftain tank.** ***Facing page, from top*** **Soviet BMP-1 APC; German 'Marder' APC; FV 439.**

vehicles both soft and armoured were distributed throughout the world with a lavish hand. The French Army were almost entirely re-equipped with American vehicles for several years, as were the Italians, and many nations who had played no part in the war were only too happy refitting their forces with Allied cast-offs. The Korean War was fought almost entirely with the same types of vehicle which had seen service in 1944-5, but that conflict served notice that these designs were reaching the end of their useful lives. Even where the vehicles still filled their designated role, they had been out of production for years, their manufacturers had turned back to other things, and spare parts were becoming increasingly expensive and difficult to obtain. It was time to start designing afresh.

One major lesson which emerged from the World War I was that infantry accompanying armour needed the protection of armour themselves. The Germans had

begun this by producing armoured half-track vehicles for their Panzer Grenadier regiments; in France and Germany, Canadian units had taken redundant self-propelled guns, stripped out the armament and turned them into armoured troop carriers, a fashion which spread rapidly through the Allied armies and served to find a useful employment for tanks when they were replaced by improved models. In the post-war years the development of APCs (Armoured Personnel Carriers) became a high priority, particularly in the light of nuclear warfare, when troops would need protection from fall-out and similar phenomena as well as from conventional weapon fire. The British Saracen was an early entrant in this field, its development having been pushed forward in order that it could be employed in Malaya; this was a six-wheeled vehicle which performed well over most sorts of terrain. The Americans, on the other hand, elected for a tracked solution and developed a number of car-

Inset, left Soviet missile carriers parading in Red Square. _Inset right_ The Soviet FROG missile on wheeled carrier/launcher vehicle. _Main picture_ Soviet multiple rocket launchers on parade.

This page, top **German 'Leopard II AV' Main Battle Tank;** ***centre*** **the Swedish 'S' tank;** ***bottom left*** **The Soviet T-72 MBT;** ***bottom right*** **the US Army's XM-1 'Abrams' MBT.** ***Facing page, top*** **American M109 self-propelled 155mm howitzer;** ***centre*** **American M110 self-propelled 175mm gun;** ***bottom left*** **French AMX 13;** ***bottom right*** **American M42 self-propelled AA gun with twin 40mm Bofors guns.**

riers before settling on the aluminium-armoured M113. This led the British to try a tracked solution, producing the Trojan series. The Soviets began with wheels, turning out a variety of formidable vehicles, and then began looking at tracks. But by that time the role of the APC had come into question; was it merely an armoured taxi-cab to take the troops to the scene of battle and drop them there, or was it to be built so that the occupants could actually fight from the vehicle? The latter point of view began to prevail in the 1960s and APCs began to sprout small turrets with heavy machine guns or small-calibre cannon, while ports in the passenger compartments allowed the occupants to fire their personal weapons while the vehicle was on the move.

The inevitable escalation followed, with different countries trying to outdo each other in the degree of protection or effectiveness of armament carried on their APCs, until the Soviets made the decisive step in 1967 by introducing a completely new class of vehicle, which has since come to be called the MICV or Mechanized

Infantry Combat Vehicle. The Soviet BMP–1 resembles a long low tank, with a midships turret carrying a 73mm gun with, above it, a launch rail for an anti-tank guided missile. But within the rear section of the hull is a passenger compartment in which eight fully-equipped infantrymen can ride, provided with their own periscopes and firing ports along the side of the hull. The vehicle is, in addition, fully amphibious. Thus it can taxi its passengers to any part of the battlefield, and can also fight very convincingly if it has to, since the armament is capable of coping with main battle tanks or virtually any other obstacle which might be met. At the present time an equivalent vehicle, the XM723, is under test with the US Army; this carries nine men in addition to the crew and will probably be armed with a 25mm cannon and two anti-tank guided missiles.

Tank development since the war has, in general, been a matter of steady development along fairly conventional lines, with the accent being placed on better armament and more sophisticated fire-control

Top left **Lightweight Land-Rover with winter camouflage in Norway.** ***Centre left*** **British Bedford 3-tonne truck, Northern Norway.** ***Bottom left*** **The Volvo over-snow articulated vehicle.**

equipment, which will ensure a high first-round-hit probability. During the war the idea of gun stabilization was pioneered; this meant using attitude sensors and mechanical gearing to ensure that once the gun was laid on to the target, it remained at the correct elevation irrespective of how the tank rocked or pitched beneath it. After the war this system was improved and was enhanced by the addition of stabilization in azimuth, so that once the gun was correctly laid and the stabilizer switched in, the barrel remained pointed at the target no matter how the tank pitched or turned. With the advent of micro-electronics it has been possible to develop small, robust computers which can be fitted inside the turret and linked to rangefinders, wind direction and speed analysers, velocity analysers, and the gun sight so as to make all the corrections necessary to compensate for meteorological conditions, target speed and angle, and ammunition characteristics and displace the gunner's aiming point accordingly, practically guaranteeing a hit. Add to this the development of infra-red night-vision equipment, image-intensifying sights, lasers and similar equipment, and it can be appreciated that

Below **Stalwart, the British Army cross-country load-carrier.** ***Upper right*** **The French AMX-30 tank recovery vehicle.** ***Lower right*** **The Chrysler XR 311 reconnaissance car, currently undergoing evaluation**

the turret of a modern tank is very full indeed.

Nevertheless, there has been room for some deviations from the general run of conventional design. When gas turbine engines appeared they were tried in tanks, though so far there have been few service applications. One such application is in the Swedish S–Tank, which broke new ground in many ways. The most notable feature of this vehicle was that the gun was fixed to the hull so that it was incapable of being elevated or traversed. To point the gun at the target, the whole tank is aligned, by raising or lowering the suspension to give elevation, and swivelling the tank on its tracks to give direction. This, of course, demands a high degree of precision in control. The advantage is that rigidly mounting the gun permits an automatic loading mechanism to be attached to the breech, which does away with the need to carry a man to load the gun. The crew is thus reduced to three men, the commander, the radioman and the driver, who, since he controls the tank, also becomes the gunner. Another advantage is that doing away with the turret allows the whole tank to be much lower and thus more easily concealed. The

Below **British Swing fire missiles are launched from Striker carriers.** *Lower left* **A Roland ground-to-air missile carrier on AMX chassis.** *Lower right* **The French Thomson-CSF Crotale missile carrier.**

disadvantage is that the gun cannot be fired while the tank is moving, and this is sufficient to condemn it in the eyes of several military critics.

For many years protection has simply meant the usual tank armour of either homogeneous or face-hardened steel. Since the war, however, it has been obvious that to gain more protection by simply adding more thickness of plate is self-defeating since the weight of the vehicle rapidly increases to the point where mobility suffers. Much work has been done on the development of aluminium armour, but this is only feasible on lightweight vehicles such as MICVs, APCs and tanks intended for carriage by air, and metallurgical considerations have argued against its use for major types of tank. In the middle 1970s the British Fighting Vehicle Experimental Establishment at Chobham announced a new system of protection called Chobham Armour. Full details of this have not been made public, but it is generally understood to be a form of laminated steel plate with ceramic interlining. This, it is claimed, defends the tank against the three methods of attack currently in use, the armour-piercing shot, the hollow charge and the squash-head shell. AP shot pierces by virtue of its kinetic energy, smashing its way through the plate; hollow charge uses a shaped charge of explosives, which, in effect, focuses the blast and bores a hole through the armour to allow blast and flame to pass into the tank; squash-head deposits a poultice of explosive on the outside of the tank and detonates it, driving a shock wave into the plate which detaches a portion of the inner face as a missile within the tank. Chobham Armour defeats these three by using the interlining; it upsets the path of a shot, smothers the penetrating jet of the hollow charge and muffles the detonating wave from squash-head. Chobham Armour has, so far, only been used on Shir Iran variations of the British Chieftain tanks and on the developing American XM–1 Abrams tank.

Soft-skinned vehicles have undergone few changes; the Jeep is still with us, though in somewhat modified form, while the Deuce-and-a-half has become the Eager Beaver, again a modification from the wartime design, but one which still betrays its ancestry. Multi-wheel, specialist high-mobility load carriers capable of keeping up with fast armoured formations are in limited use, while the Soviets have developed a wide range of specialized military trucks, in contrast to their wartime reliance on a basically civilian model. The current fashion is towards high mobility, light weight to permit air transport and engines which can operate on whatever fuel, from aviation spirit to diesel oils, that can be found.

Indeed, the same parameters can be distinguished in every facet of the military vehicle field of the present day. Only the totalitarian states can afford to be lavish with their equipment; the democracies are constantly revising their designs to keep within ever-shrinking budgets and to bestow the utmost mobility and firepower on their small but highly trained armies. As exemplified by the S-tank, if skilful design and mechanical ingenuity can save one man from a tank crew then the money spent on the design becomes worthwhile. The next few years will probably see more and more automation in combat vehicles, with automatic loaders and even more complex fire-control systems. The 1920s saw the rash of two-man tanks abandoned because the driver had his hands full and the commander had far too much to do; there is every indication that we are slowly returning to the two-man tank, now that the silicon chip and the servomotor can be harnessed into doing the routine work.